My Father Spoke Finglish at Work

VOICES OF DIVERSITY
JOHN GRABOWSKI, EDITOR

You Can't Be Mexican: You Talk Just Like Me
FRANK S. MENDEZ

My Father Spoke Finglish at Work: Finnish Americans in Northeast Ohio
EDITED BY NOREEN SIPPOLA FAIRBURN

My Father Spoke Finglish at Work

Finnish Americans in Northeast Ohio

Edited by
Noreen Sippola Fairburn

The Kent State University Press
KENT, OHIO

© 2007 by The Kent State University Press, Kent, Ohio 44242
ALL RIGHTS RESERVED
Library of Congress Catalog Card Number 2006037735
ISBN-13: 978-0-87338-909-9
ISBN-10: 0-87338-909-3
Manufactured in the United States of America

10 09 08 07 06   5 4 3 2 1

The account of Amy Kaukonen Walsh's life is a condensed version of an article researched and written by Noreen Fairburn and published in *Inland Seas: Quarterly Journal of the Great Lakes Historical Society* 46 (Winter 1990): 270–74.

LIBRARY OF CONGRESS CATALOGING-IN-PUBLICATION DATA
My father spoke Finglish at work : Finnish Americans in northeast Ohio /
edited by Noreen Sippola Fairburn.
p.   cm.—(Voices of Diversity)
ISBN-13: 978-0-87338-909-9 (hardcover : alk. paper) ∞
ISBN-10: 0-87338-909-3 (hardcover : alk. paper) ∞
1. Finnish Americans—Ohio—Ashtabula County—Biography. 2. Finnish Americans—Ohio—Ashtabula County—History—20th century. 3. Finnish Americans—Ohio—Ashtabula County—Social life and customs—20th century. 4. Immigrants—Ohio—Ashtabula County—Biography. 5. Immigrants—Ohio—Ashtabula County History—20th century. 6. Immigrants—Ohio—Ashtabula County—social life and customs—20th century. 7. Ashtabula County (Ohio)—Biography. 8. Ashtabula County (Ohio)—History—20th century. 9. Ashtabula County (Ohio)—Social life and customs—20th century.
I. Fairburn, Noreen Sippola.
F497.A73M9 2006
977.1'3400494541—dc22   2006037735

British Library Cataloging-in-Publication data are available.

Contents

Preface and Acknowledgments   vii
Introduction   xi

Late-Nineteenth-Century Arrivals, 1874–1899   1
    Martin J. Hakala   4
    Russell Holmstrom   6
    Aili (Aileen) Luoma Paulino   12
    Martin T. Ojajarvi   14
    Tellervo (Tellie) Lakari Raske Sebell   16
    Amy Kaukonen Walsh   20
    Ronald E. Korkate   22
    Kaarlo Johannas (John) Karbacka   25
    Impi Julia Maenpaa Kontas   28
    Aini (Anna) Elviira Sippola Owen   30
    Jerry Mervin (Haksluoto) Peterson   34
    Martha Viena Jarvi Ranta   37
    Mauno Johannes (John) Laituri   39
    Laina Eleanora Pouttu Sippola   43

Early-Twentieth-Century Arrivals, 1900–1909   49
    Matt Luoma   52
    Martha Lilya   55
    Arvo Johannas Ritari   57
    Ellen Susan Kesatie Sippola   59

Marilyn Ruuska Salo 62
Eugene Seline 68
Hilda Susanna Jouppila Kohta 70
Ina Maria Peaspanen Bloom 73
Oliver Kaura 76
Mamie Taanila Luoma 78
Maire (Myra) Suleima Wahlstrom 81
Allan Raymond (Ray) Keskinen 84
Laina Kahelin Dieffenbacher 87
Viena Salo Hejduk 91
Sylvia J. Holso Waltari 94
Ilona Korpela Kotila 96
Reino Johannes Saarikoski (Ray Koski) 100
Ellen Luoma Fitting 104
Mamie Wiirtanen Maki 106

Later Arrivals, 1910–1955 109
Elviira (Elvera) Sofia Koski Cherney 112
Elvi Aarnio Herlevi 115
Maynard Miles Mickelson 117
Lina Kirkkomaki (Hill) Smith 119
Ellen Edythe Salo Maxim 125
Aili Hokkonen 130
Robert Willehad Nieminen 133
Aarne E. Roivas 135
Verna J. Warpula 138
Lempi Kajander Kaihlanen 141
Eleanor Talja Andrews 143
Eino Juhannus Sinkkonen 147

Preface and Acknowledgments

These oral and written histories began as a project of the Finnish American Heritage Association of Ashtabula County (FAHA). Founded and organized in 1995 by Linda and John Riddell, the association is a group of Finnish Americans that meets monthly (excluding three winter months) to exchange stories of ancestors, celebrate Finnish holidays, and collect artifacts for their newly built Finnish American Cultural Center (FACC). Construction began on the FACC's log building in 2004, largely through the efforts of John Riddell and a volunteer crew. Assembled on the former site of Sovinto Hall, the center was completed in time for its dedication and open house, July 1, 2006.

The taped interviews were also begun in 1995, but it wasn't until 2002 that the FAHA concurred that written copies would be a better method of preserving these family stories for generations to come.

In the beginning, Marilyn Aho provided instruction for the FAHA bylaws and furnished other legal data to comply with the State of Ohio. She emphasized the importance of interviewing and recording oral histories of older Finnish Americans as an educational and permanent record of early immigrants. After attending historical seminars, Marilyn also provided a questionnaire that she adapted for this particular ethnic group. Marilyn left Ashtabula County shortly thereafter but turned over pertinent materials to Linda Sippola Riddell, who continued with the interviews.

In 1995, Linda began visiting people in their homes and in nursing residences, taking along a tape recorder and a questionnaire. Requisites were that they should be of Finnish descent and live, or have lived, in Ashtabula

County. The questions weren't always answered in precise order, and sometimes narrators strayed from the question at hand. With only one hour on each tape, additional interviews were arranged or information was gleaned from other sources such as church records and other family members.

Questionnaire
1. Who were the first persons in your family to come to the United States?
2. Where did they live in Finland, and when did they leave?
3. Do you know any stories about their journey?
4. What date did they arrive in America? Where did they first settle and find employment?
5. Where and when did your parents (or grandparents) marry?
6. When and where were you born? Do you have siblings?
7. Where did you go to school? Did you attend college? Years of graduations:
8. Was your family affiliated with a church?
9. Were Finnish traditions (foods and the sauna) and holidays observed in your home?
10. What did you do for entertainment while growing up? What chores did you have?
11. How was your family affected by the Great Depression?
12. Did you or members of your family serve during World War II?
13. Do you remember anything about the Finnish halls, parks, or stores?
14. Who did you marry and when?
15. Name your children and give birth dates:
16. How did you earn a living? Was your spouse employed?
17. When, and from where, did you or your spouse retire?
18. Have you ever traveled to Finland?
19. Have you received any awards, honors, or special recognition?
20. What changes have you observed in your community and in the world?
21. Tell about anything humorous or tragic, or of general interest during any period in your life.

In response, a few outlined or wrote their own memoirs, and one interview was conducted over the telephone. Rebecca (Niemi) Sloan first began transcribing and typing the oral stories, but her work as a journalist for the (Youngstown) *Vindicator*, along with her family responsibilities, left no time to continue this additional task. Beginning in January 2005, Linda Riddell transcribed the remainder, typing them verbatim; she then gave these copies to me. I edited and arranged each interview in chronological order and, after additional research, I compiled the following material.

The first-person accounts were written as the narrator told them with the exception of minor alterations for the sake of clarity; brackets enclose further explanations. Some photos were donated to the Finnish American Heritage Association, some were loaned by family members, and some were loaned by a private collector. Thus, this project has been a collaborative effort from its inception.

The following oral and written histories are a mere sampling of Finnish Americans in Ashtabula County and its environs; nevertheless, they may prompt others, whatever their ethnic background, to record their own family histories for generations to come.

This publication would never have been initiated if it had not been for the Finnish descendants who consented to share their families' stories. Many were in their eighties or nineties at the time of their interviews, yet their memories of days gone by were told with frankness and clarity. We give our heartfelt thanks to those still with us and regret that those who have passed on during the many years when the interviewing and publishing were underway will not get to see their contributions in print.

Thanks and gratitude must be expressed to the many people who contributed additional information or photos of a parent or spouse: Janis Bloom Eldridge, Joanne Fitting Carpenter, Susan Luoma Rose, Elizabeth Karbacka, Eleanor Kaihlanen Stevenson, Katherine Kaura, Betty Kohta Wormley, Rhoda Korkate, Maxine Koski, Sonja Kotila Corlew, Elaine Raaske Richardson, Glenn Sippola, Rebecca Niemi Sloan, and Will Fitzhugh, founder and editor of the *Concord Review*.

Many thanks to Rita Hjerpe, program director, Bethany Lutheran Church, who graciously answered questions and provided from files and ledgers the dates and other pertinent information necessary for clarification and accuracy.

Thanks, also, to Dee Riley, photographer, for her expert help and advice; and to Doree Petros for generously lending select photos from her extensive family collection.

And a special thanks to my husband, Robert Fairburn, who is more computer savvy than I am. He solved technical problems that spared me from frustration and anxiety.

Thanks and appreciation also go to Joanna Hildebrand Craig, assistant director/editor-in-chief, Kent State University Press, with whom I corresponded initially and who encouraged me through the entire book-publishing process. Gratitude must be expressed to John J. Grabowski, Voices of Diversity series editor; Will Underwood, director of Kent State University Press; Tara C. Lenington, project editor; Christine Brooks, design and production manager; Susan Cash, marketing manager; and to any other member of the editorial board who voted unanimously to accept this manuscript for publication.

Introduction

Although Finns came with Swedes to Delaware as early as 1638, the first permanent settlement of Finns in Ashtabula Harbor, Ohio, wasn't established until 1874 when a small crew arrived to work as ore shovelers on the Hanna Docks. Immigration accelerated to this area in the late nineteenth and early twentieth centuries. In 1891 the number of Finland-born in Ashtabula was 1,300, and by 1938 they numbered more than 4,000. They came to Ashtabula and to other Lake Erie port towns, such as Conneaut and Fairport Harbor, where there was heavy manual labor working on the railroads or loading and unloading ships that plied the Great Lakes. The hours were long and the wages low, but these stalwart immigrants struggled on to send passage to family waiting in Finland and to buy homes once their families arrived. Women or children occasionally traveled alone, in most instances to join family already here. And there were those who yearned for farmland and may have worked on the docks or the railroads only until they had earned enough to buy land and move to rural areas.

They emigrated from Finland for various reasons. The population in Finland had grown considerably by 1900, and there was little employment available, especially for younger siblings when, by tradition, the oldest son inherited the family farm. More often they were crofters, or farm tenants, with no hope of owning land. In 1899, when Finland was still a duchy under the Russian czar, Russia's grip tightened in many aspects of their lives. For example, the Russian language was to be used in government and education, and men were to be conscripted into Russia's army. The Finns' protests were ignored, so, rather than yielding to Russia's demands, many left the country around the beginning of the twentieth century.

Of those included in this volume, only one was well-educated and emigrated from Helsinki, Finland's largest city. One other came from Tampere, and one came from Sortavala, which is now a part of Russia. With the exception of the one from Helsinki, all were of the working class, and most hailed from small villages or farms in the province of Vaasa (now southern Ostrobothnia), which borders the Gulf of Bothnia and stretches inland toward central Finland, and from Oulu province, north of Vaasa.

Thus, they came for economic or political reasons, and when letters arrived from those who emigrated earlier, telling of the comparatively good wages and opportunities in America, this was also persuasive. They settled in areas where they knew other Finns and where the climate was similar to Finland, such as the states surrounding the Great Lakes. They clustered in the same areas, with the hope of retaining their language and customs among fellow countrymen. Although surnames may be the same, the families may not necessarily be related, for individuals and families adopted the surname of the farm owner wherever they last held tenancy. Once here, some surnames were anglicized, and children often changed their first names because of shame or embarrassment with their foreign-sounding, often mispronounced names in schools.

Other than a small trunk of personal belongings, they also brought their language, religion, love of music, and traditions. They built their saunas, celebrated Finnish holidays, cooked familiar Finnish foods, and endured disappointments and tragedies with an innate trait the Finns call *sisu,* a word not easily defined because it has many connotations. It is the indomitable will that makes Finns endure when stamina is needed in work, war, or athletics. It is inner strength that sustains them in the face of adversity. When Finns are challenged in countless ways throughout their lifetimes, they remind themselves to use their *sisu* by persevering with patience and fortitude and by keeping their faith.

Learning the English language for those immigrating as adults was especially difficult. Finnish bears no resemblance to the languages of neighboring Sweden or Russia. It does, however, have Roman roots, so the alphabet is similar to the English form, except that it has only nineteen letters and relies heavily on vowels rather than consonants. Their language also has no articles or future tense, and the accent is always on the first syllable. The men, out of necessity, had to learn enough English to succeed in their jobs, but their attempts at speaking the new language resulted in a combination of Finnish and English that became known as "Finglish." Ashtabula, for example, is a native Indian word loosely translated as "fish river." In Finglish this word is pronounced US'-te-pulla. Most women continued to speak their native language for the remainder of their lives. The children, however, quickly learned English upon entering American schools, even though Finnish was still the primary language in the homes until the Finland-born generation passed away.

Perhaps it was the second generation who had the more difficult role, keeping one foot in their parents' generation while stepping with the other into American culture. This generation wanted to learn the new language, become educated, and, in general, have a more prosperous life than their hard-working parents who clung to the old-country ways. This generation coped while growing up during the Depression years, often serving in World War II, either in the military or on the home front. The second generation most often married other Finns who lived in the same neighborhoods and attended the same schools and social events. Moreover, their parents frowned upon marriages to those who were not Finnish and who were not of the same religious persuasion.

In the early decades of the twentieth century, the Finns were the largest ethnic group in Ashtabula, followed by Italians, Swedes, and then the Irish. As time went on, all groups became less clannish and began to intermingle, and the unwritten family rule was overlooked when they began to marry more frequently outside their own nationality. Today, even the Lutheran churches established by the early Finns are no longer Finnish strongholds.

Late-Nineteenth-Century Arrivals, 1874–1899

A small crew of Finnish men first arrived in Ashtabula Harbor in 1872 to complete construction of the northern leg of the Pittsburgh, Youngstown, and Ashtabula Railroad (PY&A). This railroad was necessary to transport coal north from the Pennsylvania coal mines and to ship iron ore south from the mines in Minnesota and Michigan's Upper Peninsula to the Pittsburgh and Youngstown steel mills. When the railroad was completed in 1873, this Finnish crew moved on, but in 1874 another group arrived to work as ore shovelers at the Hanna Dock, and a permanent settlement was begun. There were few women among them in those early years, for single men or married men usually arrived first to earn enough passage for siblings or wives.

The first method of loading coal onto boats was by pushing wheelbarrows up a gangplank and dumping them. To unload ore, one-ton buckets were lowered into the boat's hold while men inside filled the buckets with their shovels. As if these ten-hour days, seven days a week weren't enough to endure, the living conditions were less than accommodating. Cramped boarding houses were the norm, with outhouses in the backyards. There was no shortage of work, however, and thousands of several ethnic groups were employed.

At the docks, there were no coffee breaks; instead, kegs of beer were hauled in to slacken the workers' thirst. Gang bosses often paid their crews with silver coins while they congregated in a saloon. These coins were often spent in the saloons, while old-country "Martta's" promised passage was temporarily forgotten. When the boats took days to load or unload, sailors also frequented the saloons, resulting in fighting and gambling. Houses of ill repute also appeared, adding to the degradation.

During the ensuing years, as more women arrived carrying their Bibles and hymn books, changes were made to ameliorate these conditions. As mechanization was gradually developed at the docks, working hours were reduced or men were laid off. Many were then forced to seek other means of supporting their growing families such as ship-building, maintaining small businesses, or buying that long-yearned-for farm.

Martin J. Hakala

My father is believed to be the first Finnish baby born in Ashtabula Harbor. His name was John Hakala, born in 1876. I don't know my grandparents' names, but I had three uncles and one aunt on my father's side. My mother's name was Sofie Poltto, and she was born on a farm in Raahe, Finland. They had tough times then, and my mother believed the streets in America were paved with gold. So she traveled to this country in steerage class and settled in Ashtabula Harbor.

My folks met and were married in Ashtabula. They had five children: Nelma was the oldest, then Gertrude. Another girl died in infancy. Then there were the three boys: Carl, Paul, and me. I was born on February 22, 1904. At that time they lived on Oak Street [West Eighth Street] in a house that had a bathtub and an inside toilet. [In 1930, most streets in Ashtabula were changed from names to numbers, and the Ashtabula River divided the east and west sides.]

My dad worked at the Hanna Docks as an operator of a machine that unloaded ships; he sometimes worked at night.

Before bedtime, my mother used to tell us stories about Finland. I remember the Bloomquists lived next door. We went to the Finnish Congregational Church at the corner of Oak and Coyne. They used to call it the "little church," and I think some people looked down on it. We went to Washington [Elementary] School, then to Harbor High.

We had wonderful parents when we were growing up. Christmas was wonderful when we had special things to eat. My mother cooked meat and potatoes, and we liked her *reikäleipä* [rye bread]. We used to buy some baked goods at Jack Sippola's bakery. I remember how Mrs. Sippola would always be sweeping the sidewalk off in front of the bakery. Three brothers had a grocery store called Lampela Brothers. On the lower end of Oak Street was a toggery shop owned by Salgen, and John Hummer had a dry-goods store. He was a sort of "Keystone Cop" kind of guy. He had a beer wagon, and he would pull up with his horses, and say, "What's your name? I'm a Finn—John Hummer." The grocery stores were mostly east of Joseph Avenue. I remember High Street [Morton Drive] were the bars [saloons] were parallel to the river. Oak Street also had Dublin House—a boarding house—and there was a saloon in there, too. Hank Kinnunen built seven homes in a row on Joseph Avenue that we called *Kinnunen Kaupunki* [Kinnunen's Town]. These were across from the old Bethany Lutheran Church, and they named them after the days of the week: Monday to Sunday, but the Wednesday house burned down.

My first job as a youngster was weeding onions in a greenhouse. I made eighty cents for eight hours. When the schools were closed during the 1918 influenza epidemic, I worked as a rivet-passer in the shipyards and made thirty-seven and a half cents an hour. I worked on the docks as a weigh master in summers, and I once worked at a feed store on Bridge Street; that store later moved to Lake Avenue.

Some Finns kept cows to get milk, and there was a pasture near the overhead bridge on West Nineteenth called Brown's pasture. There was a water trough on the corners of Lake Avenue and Oak Street. That was fun when you had to step over cow pies or get your feet warmed up! My dad worked once on a farm, west of Haywood Beach, and our family would camp there most of the summer. We cooked outside in their apple orchard.

My father was lucky during the Depression, since he worked as an operator at the docks. I remember the soup kitchens that were formed, and some of the churches served meals. People who couldn't afford to buy coal went to the coal yards at the docks and picked up lumps of coal during the night. The next day they would say, "We went blackberrying last night." Then railroad cops would whitewash the tops of coal piles so they could detect stolen coal, but scrapings and fine coal were often given to dock employees, and it could be hauled for a dollar a load.

After I graduated from high school in 1922, I went to Spencerian Business College in Cleveland for two years. I worked first as a manager of deposits at the Harbor Building and Loan. Me and Richard Ranta (Senior) were responsible for starting that company. We did better with real estate [loans] than they did uptown on Main Street. During the Depression, we lost money, but I helped clean up the losses and then got savings insured. Things got better during the Depression when the WPA [Works Progress Administration] was organized. They paved some Ashtabula streets and expanded the city sewers. Peoples Savings and Loan bought out Harbor Building and Loan, but I was able to stay on with them as a manager. I was never out of work.

I remember all the halls: Socialist halls, and Sovinto [Harmony] Hall—the biggest wooden hall—with a wonderful dance floor. They had live music with polkas and folk music. They had Finnish plays and I acted in them in the 1930s. They had the Sovinto Male Chorus, and I sang with them, all in Finnish. The athletic groups were wonderful, with baseball and basketball. I remember every Thursday was the maids' day off, so there were always dances at Sovinto on Thursdays.

I married Ina Niemi on August 12, 1930. She grew up in Fitchburg, Massachusetts, and had come to Ashtabula to visit relatives, and that's how I met her. We had two daughters: Joan [Lorentzen], born in 1931; and Karen [Haussman], born in 1934. We bought a house on Michigan Avenue in the Harbor. I went to the public saunas, one or the other, three times a week: Wednesdays, Fridays, and Saturdays. Next to my wife, I loved a sauna best.

We belonged to Bethany Lutheran Church, and my wife and I both sang in the choir. I sang in the Town Choir, too, as it was first the Sovinto Chorus. And I belonged to the Harbor [Mason's] Lodge, El Kadir, and the North End Club. I retired from Peoples after working there forty-five years.

We had been married fifty-three years when my wife died in 1985; she was seventy-eight years old. Both our girls live in California, so I later moved into the Country Club Retirement Campus.

Martin died at the age of ninety-one on June 26, 1995.

Russell Holmstrom

My grandfather, Oscar Ferdinand Holmstrom, was the first one in my family to come to this country. He was from Summinkylä, and he came to Ashtabula Harbor in 1888, when he was eighteen. He traveled with his two brothers and three Holmstrom cousins. My grandfather married Edla Gran, who came to this country from Ylistaro, in about 1890. They were married in 1892 in the Finnish Congregational Church by Reverend Franz Lehtinen.

My Holmstrom grandfather learned carpentry in Ashtabula. He built his own house on Cherry Street [West Ninth Street] in 1898 and built the parsonage for the first Bethany Lutheran Church, the one on the corner of Joseph Avenue and West Eighth Street.

On my mother's side, my grandmother's name was Maija [Mary] Karhu. She came here with her sister. They were the two children of my great-grandfather's second marriage. His first marriage was to Emma, and they had four children, but three of them died when they were young. My great-grandfather married the third time, this time to a woman fifteen or twenty years younger. Her name was Evelina Skiff, and they had four children. Two lived to be adults: Senia and Liisa. I met those two in Finland on my second trip over there, and they lived about five years after that—in their middle eighties. Senia was married twice and had no children, and Liisa had five daughters.

My grandmother said it was a very bad trip here, and she couldn't eat anything but oranges and crackers. My grandfather never told me too much about his background, except that he came from Ylihärmä. His name was Antti Maki. Then he changed it to Hill at the time of taking his citizenship papers. There was just too many Makis, and they got everything confused in the mail. There was Antti Maki, Heikki Maki, and another, and you name it. That's the reason we have Makis and we have Hills ["Maki" means "hill" in Finnish].

I don't know why the Holmstroms came here, but it was probably a plan of the six Holmstroms—three brothers and three cousins. The two brothers were Arthur and Edward. Edward lived in Erie, Pennsylvania, and raised a family. He worked in Erie on the railroad, and that's where he died. Arthur lived here about five years, then he went back to Finland. I met him there in 1952. He lived to be the age of eighty-eight, but he didn't have children and was married twice. The cousins, Walter and Mikko, they went to Erie. Frank, he stayed in Ashtabula, and he's the one that played the organ at Bethany Church. That was Esther Karkutt's father. He was married three times. His first marriage he had Toivo and Tynne, then the second time he married his wife's sister. Then, when she died, he got a girl from Finland whose was Maria Vahanen. She was Esther's mother. She was the only child of that marriage.

In 1894 my grandmother's [Edla Gran] mother was ailing, so she asked her two daughters to come and visit before she died, and they did. And I don't know how many months it was, and then she died, and they got their inheritance money and came back to the U.S.A. They were married in the U.S.A., and each one had a baby at that time.

My father, Paul Oscar Holmstrom, was born in his parents' home on Cherry Street in Ashtabula. My mother was born on Day Street in Conneaut. Her name was Aini, but she went by Inez Elizabeth Hill. My grandfather [Hill] worked at the docks in Conneaut, then in later years on the railroad. In 1905 he moved to Cherry Hill, Pennsylvania, and had a fifty-acre farm. That's where he had his family: eleven children, but only seven lived to adulthood—six boys and one girl [Inez].

My sister, Edith, was the oldest, born in 1922, then I was born on June 21, 1924, in Nystrom's Maternity Hospital on West Eighth Street. It's a terrible looking house today, but in those days I guess it was okay. I was born during one of the worst storms from Sandusky to Buffalo. And fifty years after that it was printed in the *News Herald,* like they reprint the stories, and it said it was the worst storm along the lake—on the first day of summer. My brother, Bill, was three years younger than me, and my brother, Harold, was eight years younger than I was.

Our family lived in Detroit, Akron, and Port Clinton, but most of the time in Ashtabula Harbor. I went to Washington School and to Bethany Lutheran Church. My Holmstrom grandparents were charter members of Bethany.

My grandfather built his second house in 1925, and in 1931 we moved in with them. My grandmother fell on the basement steps and broke her hip, so we moved in to take care of her. She died in 1933.

Most of the time we went to Cherry Hill for Christmas on the farm, and they didn't have electricity there until 1932. We used to go to the woods to get the Christmas trees, and they didn't have those great, nice pines. They had those hemlocks, and we'd get three trees and wrap them together to make one nice tree out of it. I can recall when they put lighted candles in the windows. When Mother was a girl, they had lighted candles on the tree, and they had to watch them very closely. They just lit them on Christmas Eve. On New Year's Eve, we used to take hot lead in a dipper and drop it in cold water to get our fortunes for the next year [a tradition predating Christianity]. My mother told me that, when she was a young girl, her brother Carl's lead turned out like a little coffin, and he died there that year at the age of five. He had diphtheria and died in my grandmother's arms. He said, "Mother, I'm going home to the angels."

We used to have church meetings out in the country because it was too far to go into town. We'd meet at different people's houses. There was a lot of Finnish families in Clark's Corners, Brown's Corners, and Cherry Hill. I have a picture of about fifty people at one of these church meetings. I remember once Grandma got very overheated on a hot summer day and they had to put her to bed.

My mother made liver loaf with raisins, the same way her mother and mother-in-law made it. You never ate more than about a tablespoon because it was so darn rich. And she made rutabaga loaf with cracker crumbs and stuff and salmon loaf and salmon patties. And they made a Finnish salad with beets, carrots, potatoes, and green onions. A lot of Finnish people liked it with fish, but the younger people didn't like *lipeäkala* [dried cod] because they used to soak it in lye water for many days and it wasn't very appetizing. So they usually just made roast beef.

The oldest thing I have is a china water pitcher; it was given to my grandparents on their wedding day from Reverend Lehtinen and his wife. I also have my grandmother's 1910 slag-glass shade, and the lamp is bronze. I gave it to my daughter. I had a shelf that my grandfather made to hang cups and saucers on, and I gave that to my brother Harold. Then I had a little cabinet that belonged to my grandfather. It had a hole in the top where you put the bowl and pitcher, and it had a little compartment underneath where you could hide your money. My uncle Ray had it for a while, and that's where he hid his money. I finally gave it to my daughter Lisa.

I had so many pictures, and I couldn't identify some of them, so I took them to the County Home, where those elderly people could recognize some of them. I kept those, but the ones I didn't know, I sold. People do buy old pictures. I think what they want is a family, so they create a family for themselves.

Sovinto Hall was around the corner from us. They used to have dances, political programs, roller-skating, and boxing. Behind the hall was the band's hall, where they practiced. That was a stone's throw from where we lived. There was five Finnish churches at one time in the Harbor. One church met in the people's house, and I don't know what they call that, but the building was called Olavanlinna, like the big castle in Finland. They had four apartments there, and they had a charismatic service where they would speak in tongues. I would listen, but I didn't know what they were saying, and they probably didn't know because they were speaking in tongues.

The Modern Woodmen of America [a fraternal order] would meet at Woodmen Park on Lake Road where the CEI [Cleveland Electric Illuminating Co.] property is. Some of that property belonged to my father's cousin, Hilda Gran. She was a nurse in World War I, and they gave her a shot in the spine and it paralyzed her. She was in a wheelchair for the rest of her life. I saw her last time in 1950, in southern California. She lived in a three-room apartment, and she had a woman to drive her around, but she couldn't go too much. She gave us a ticket to go to Knott's Berry Farm for a dinner.

We didn't go to Haywood Beach. That was called "sin swamp." There was three kinds of Finns in Ashtabula: There was the "whites"; they were the church people. The "yellow" were Socialists, and the "reds" were Communists. My grandparents didn't like the Communists. And one woman never liked my mother because she was a church person. There was a lot of kids whose folks were Socialists, but I didn't pay too much attention. They were fence-sitters. They didn't know whether to jump off the fence and go to church, or jump off the fence and go to the "red" side.

I had an old picture of the *Humina* [Murmur] Band when Williamson was the director. His daughter was a vocalist in it. They were quite high toned. She had a feather boa around her neck and a long dress. They were one of the best musical groups in that area. Conneaut had a lot of musical groups, too, in Kilpi Hall [now Conneaut Community Center]. My grandmother, Edla, had a brother, Konstaa Gran. When he came to this country he settled in Conneaut. He was an architect and drew the plans for Kilpi Hall, and he was the master carpenter. They made a widow's walk at the top, but that's before my time. They took it [widow's walk] down when it weakened. Behind Kilpi Hall was a little confectionery store owned by my great-grandfather. His name was Karhu, the second husband of my great-grandmother, Liisa. Her first husband was Matti Maki, and she was married about five years to him. He was going down the road in Finland and the horse and buggy overturned. He and the horse were killed in the accident. So she had to go out and work in a little town—Verdi—sort of a Swedish settlement, and she put her kids as shepherds among her relatives. My grandfather was a cabin boy at the age of ten on a Swedish boat. Both of my grandparents spoke Swedish, because you had to in order to get along. My grandmother used to talk a little bit of Swedish, and I didn't know that she was talking Swede, because when you're a kid you don't question. I never made the connection until I became an adult.

Grandfather Holmstrom was a very pious church person. In fact, some of his relatives in Finland are what you would call Amish. My grandmother would say it's a big deal to go to school. My parents had to pay; it wasn't free. My grandfather Hill was poor as a church mouse, but he could still read the newspaper. You know why? He went to confirmation school, and you had to learn how to read then.

Sippola Bakery was a Conneaut bakery, and they were also in Ashtabula. Later, Talvola's was in there, and they used to make that rye bread with a hole in it. John Maki was my father's friend, and he was a bachelor who painted houses. He also taught citizenship classes. When he died, my father took over his classes. My dad was always telling us kids stories. He worked at Bjerstedt's Bakery and would be making cream puffs and lady fingers. Once the window was open and he saw the Swedish preacher walking by with a big stovepipe hat, and he threw a cream puff at him, then said to his friend: "I got to go to the restroom; will you take over for me?"

On Halloween we went into a neighbor's milk house and grabbed his wagon. It was real light—a one-horse wagon. We'd go down the road and he'd have the cops waiting for us. When the cops got close, we'd run into the woods.

My first job was cleaning furnaces and putting new parts in. That was a dirty, dirty old job. I was eighteen and got fifty cents an hour. Before that, I worked for my grandfather Holmstrom, and he paid me thirty-five cents to help him in carpenter work.

We lived on High Street in Conneaut during the Depression. We were fortunate because my father had a degree in chemical engineering and worked away from home in Columbus. But it was very hard for large families, and you wondered how they made out. You could go down to the Harbor fire station and get a bowl of soup, a cup of milk, and a slice of bread. One lady went there three times a day, and I was surprised because I didn't know they could do that. This one widow lady got on welfare, and she was afraid to stay alone at night, so she paid me a quarter to stay over there. She told me I could eat breakfast for a quarter, but I thought I'd go home and eat and save my quarter. One family down the street was in a bad way. They had eight children. My father managed to speak on behalf of one girl who had a business education, and she was able to work for the State of Ohio in an office. Her wages kept that family going.

I remember my only birthday party at the age of twelve. My mother bought a three-tiered, white cake that cost one dollar, and that was a great thing. I remember what I got: two pairs of socks, two handkerchiefs, and a pint of peanuts.

During World War II, I worked on State Road for the American Fork and Hoe bayonet factory. Lots of Ashtabula Finns worked there, too. I bought my first car; it was a 1928 Chevy, and I paid twenty-five dollars for it. I drove it to Conneaut, and on the way I had about four flat tires. I sold it to my uncle for twenty-five dollars, and he fixed it up and sold it for over a hundred dollars.

The neighborhoods in Ashtabula have changed. There were no houses in what we called the "squirrel woods." Bethany Church bought fourteen lots there when they were cheap. Now homes stretch all the way to Kent [State] University and along. Beyond, that was all open country. When I was a kid there was houses here and there, but not very many. The most settled place was Ashtabula Harbor, where we could walk to the stores.

Konstaa [Gran] helped build the Masonic Temple and the Mother of Sorrows Church in Ashtabula. His son Charles, also a builder, constructed gas stations at Five Points and at Bunker Hill. One gas station was on the site where Garfield's Restaurant now stands. Another son, Bill, made so much money while building the Reliance Electric plant that he retired at forty-eight and went to visit relatives in Florida. When he came back, his car skidded on the road near Geneva, and he was admitted to the hospital. But he wasn't x-rayed and was in pretty bad shape. They took him to Hotel Ashtabula, and that's where his son found him unconscious. He died at the age of forty-eight.

I married Mary Elizabeth (Betty) Blood in 1957. We have two daughters: Holly, born in 1959, and Lisa, born in 1961. We lived on High Street in Conneaut when the girls were born.

When Russell visited Finland he brought back some wooden items, two of which he donated to the Finnish American Heritage Association (FAHA): a calf's restraint, designed to prevent a calf from going through a fence; and a rug beater. He also donated a bread receiver, used for lifting hot bread from the oven, which his grandmother Hill made in the early 1900s. Russell and Betty are retired, and live on Lake Road in Conneaut.

Aili (Aileen) Luoma Paulino

My mother, Aili Kustaava Hannula, was born in Alavieska, Finland, in the Oulu Province. Her brother was in Ashtabula, and he sent her the money for passage to America. My father, August Luoma, came from Laupua and Nurmo, in the Vaasa region, and came here sometime in the 1880s.

My mother worked as a maid in a boarding house, and that's where she met my father. They were married sometime in the early 1890s. My father worked for the New York Central Railroad, and they first lived on Pine Street [West Fourth Street]. My brother William was their first son, born on April 2, 1894; then my sisters, Sophie (Porkala), and Sallie (Schiff); then Arthur, who was born on October 5, 1899. I was the youngest, born on March 26, 1903. Arthur was killed when he was only twenty-one. He attempted to hop a train headed for Erie, Pennsylvania, and got one leg cut off.

When we moved to Iowa Street [Lyndon Avenue], I went to the brick school called Farmdale on Carpenter Road. I went to Harbor High School, but I didn't finish my last year. Instead, I went into nurses' training at Ashtabula General Hospital. They wanted someone there who could speak two languages, so I became an interpreter for Finnish patients and their doctors. Jennie Johnson was the other Finn nurse, but she worked different hours than I did. I got real high grades, and I became a registered nurse in 1927 after some more training at Mount Sinai Hospital in Cleveland.

We went to the Finnish Congregational Church, which was called "the little church," but I later joined Bethany Lutheran Church, which was called "the big church," and I was baptized there when I was older. I went to different programs at Sovinto Hall, and I especially liked to go there for New Year's Eve celebrations. We always went to a public sauna on *Juhannus* [St. John's Day, or the summer solstice].

After I grew up, during the 1920s, I attended different functions for nurses. My mother was very religious and wanted no part of anything not connected with the church. So I kept a change of clothes in a shed we had behind our house. Then I would change my clothes there and sneak away to meet other girls to go to a movie house or to Woodland Beach Park—the old amusement park.

I met my husband, Herc Paulino, on the third floor of Hotel Adamson on Bridge Street. At that time, Herc was a young attorney with the law firm of Dunlavy and Goggin. I had stayed four nights giving nursing care to Mrs. Adamson, so I was called in to witness her will. I had on a real nice dress and my long hair was fixed real nice, and Herc asked when he could see me again. I said, "How about Saturday night?" He agreed, and after that we saw each other two or three times a week. He had a Model-T Ford that we drove around in.

Herc and I were married in 1929. I was twenty-six, and Herc was twenty-eight. We had three children: Harry, born in 1930; Mary Jane, born in 1932; and James in 1935. I stayed home and took care of my family during the Depression. In those days they believed a wife shouldn't work outside the home. I did some relief work at the hospital, though, and during World War II I worked as an industrial nurse at the Electrometallurgical Plant in Ashtabula. Herc was too young for World War I and too old to be in World War II.

Governor Frank J. Lausche appointed my husband Ashtabula Municipal Court Judge in 1946, and he kept that position for twenty-three years. We had a nice life and traveled a lot. We went to Finland twice and to India with the Reliance Travel Club. Traveling was reasonably priced in those days. We were members of St. Joseph Church in Ashtabula.

Herc died suddenly in 1969. He had to go to a meeting in Columbus, so I went along so we could visit our son Harry, who lived in Columbus. We had just finished dinner and Herc was playing with our grandchildren when he had a heart attack and died right then and there. It shocked all of us. Ashtabula's city manager closed the city offices on the day of Herc's funeral.

Judge Herc Paulino died on September 4, 1969, at age sixty-eight. At the time of Herc Paulino's death, he and Aileen had been married forty years. She never remarried. Aileen spent her last years at the Country Club Retirement Campus in Ashtabula. At the time of her interview she was ninety-five years old. When asked to what she attributed her long life, she replied: "I just live one day at a time." At the time of her death, on January 30, 2003, she was two months shy of her 100th birthday. In addition to her three children, she was survived by eleven grandchildren and seventeen great-grandchildren.

Martin T. Ojajarvi

My father, Kalle (Charles) Ojajarvi, came to America around 1890. He emigrated from Alajärvi because of poverty in Finland, and went to Conneaut, Ohio. When his first wife died, they had three girls and one boy; that was his first family. My dad didn't know anyone in Conneaut when he first came.

My mother's name was Liisa Sammalisto, and she came from a small town called Nurmo—near Seinäjoki. She had sisters and brothers in Conneaut, so that's where she went. She met and married my dad in Conneaut, and they lived on Broad Street. I had three older brothers: Charles, George, and Reino. I was born on September 29, 1921.

I grew up in Monroe Township and went to Kelloggsville Elementary School and Monroe School for the first eight years. Then I went to Kingsville High School for two years but finished at Rowe High School in Conneaut. In Kelloggsville, I went to a two-room school. One room was used for classes, and the other one for an ice rink. We used to put water on the floor in that part, and it would stay frozen for a long time because the sun didn't hit it. We had our private skating rink—no skates, just an ice rink. It was a good play area, too, when it was bad weather outdoors. I rode a kid hack for about four or five years. When the roads were good they used a Model-T truck, and when it got bad weather, they used either a bobsled or wagon. There weren't any snowplows at all them days.

We moved to the Kinnunen farm in Kelloggsville during the Depression. My dad had a butter-and-egg route between Conneaut and Ashtabula at that time. Every Saturday he went to Conneaut, and on Wednesdays, or twice a month, he went to Ashtabula. We didn't need food assistance then.

My first job was being a water boy in 1936. When they were widening Route 20, east of Conneaut, I had to carry two pails of water and one dipper for the workers. No cups at all in those days.

The only time we celebrated Christmas was when the youngest sister from my dad's first family became a schoolteacher in Youngstown, and she brought home a tree. The only traditions we kept up of Finnish was that we went to the Finnish Lutheran Church on Broad Street, and we took a sauna wherever we could find one. My dad never had one for us. One time we had a *Juhannus* bonfire at Elonen's farm. I remember they came from Farnham with three fire trucks to put out the fire. They ordered everybody off of Route 7 because they had so many calls about the fire. The fire company didn't know what was what.

My mother's mainstay was cooking *mojakka,* that Finnish stew, and she made rice pudding. She baked her bread from all grain, all stone-ground from Fuller's Mill in Farnham.

Kilpi Hall was the place to go in Conneaut. It was a temperance hall, and they had one Sunday a month for an afternoon church service there. They had an athletic club, but I wasn't old enough to belong. The pastor also came out to the country in Kelloggsville, and we met at the Kinnunen farm, the one where we lived. Hatches Corners Road had an old one-room schoolhouse, and Reverend Harju came to that. That building is still standing, but it has had some alterations made, like a garage door put on the side of it. It's a nice turn-of-the-century small building with a Victorian-trimmed front door.

The only park we went to was Lakeview Park. It was behind Kilpi Hall and overlooked the lake. It had a nice old building used for dancing, and roller skating for the kids to enjoy. I remember it being painted a sage-green color. We had different water holes where we went swimming, even at the new covered-bridge site on State Line Road.

I remember my dad wore some skis during a bad winter. My one brother made the skis. They were real flexible and extra long—taller than me, about seven or eight feet long. My dad went with those skis cross lots to get to the Bushnell store to buy groceries. It was the big snow storm of 1944, and Furnace Road didn't get plowed out for three months. He even backpacked to carry the stuff for two other Finnish families, Makis and Orrenmaas. He used the skis quite a bit to get to a gas well, too, because he didn't have a tractor to get back there.

I was in the air force in Europe in World War II. My oldest brother [Charles] got killed, then my brother Reino, so they said I'd be sent home, but they lost my records and I didn't get out until three or four months later in November. I was traveling from Germany on discharge papers sent from a letter they sent to my home. I had three battle stars on my uniform when I got discharged, but I don't know if they got lost or what.

I married Vivian Bebout in 1951, and we lived at the old homestead in Kelloggsville. We never had children, but my wife already had one daughter and one son. I went to work on construction as a laborer through the union hall in Ashtabula. We were allowed to salvage lumber, but we weren't allowed to construct anything with it.

What changed the most in Conneaut was that Main Street stores have disappeared. There aren't hardly any stores there anymore. In the country there is a lot more idle land than there ever was, and very few dairy farms.

Martin retired in 1983 after nineteen years at Lawler, Inc./Carlson Steel. His later years were spent in an apartment on Harbor Street in Conneaut. He was a member of the State Line United Methodist Church, the Loyal Order of Moose, and the Veterans of Foreign Wars. Martin died on September 22, 2003, at the age of eighty-one. He was preceded in death by his wife Vivian, a half-brother, and four half-sisters. Martin made provisions in his will for donations to the State Line United Methodist Church and to the FAHA.

Tellervo (Tellie) Lakari Raske Sebell

My paternal grandfather, Matti Lakari, was fifty years old when he left Isokyro—in the Vaasa province of Finland—to immigrate to America in 1890. His wife, Maria, and their five sons—Matti, age fifteen; John, age twelve; Emil, nine; Edward, four; and Walter, one—were left behind until he could send for them later. Matti had been forced to sell his farm to cover debts on a note he had signed, so when he left, Maria and her five sons moved into a small cottage on her parents' farm.

Newberry, Michigan, is believed to be Matti's first stop because he had a photograph taken there of himself in 1890. From there he went with a group of other Finnish men to Carbon, Wyoming, where the Union Pacific Railroad was operating a coal mine. But before he could send money for his family's passage, he was killed in a mining accident in 1894. He was buried in a mass, unmarked grave in Carbon. Carbon is now a ghost town. So that's why Maria never left Finland, but her son, Edward, later settled in Canada, and Emil and Walter eventually settled in the United States.

My maternal grandfather was Robert Glantz. His surname was originally Ojala, but it was changed to Glantz when his mother remarried after the death of his father in 1887. My grandfather was thirty-one when he left Seinäjoki, where he had worked on a large farming estate. It was on that farm where he met his wife, Maria, who worked there as a dairymaid.

Robert and Maria were married and had two children. John was five, and Aino, eighteen months, when they emigrated from Finland in 1893. They settled in Ashtabula Harbor, where they knew other Finns, and my grandfather found work at the docks shoveling coal.

My father, Walter Lakari, was born in 1889, the youngest of Matti's sons. He didn't have much formal education and, at one time, had worked as a shepherd boy on a neighboring farm. He came to America in 1907, when he was about eighteen. He first traveled around the country, trying to find work wherever it was available, but he kept learning English and American customs as he went along. He sent postcards to his brother Emil from Scofield, Utah, with pictures of the mine where he worked. Other cards were sent from Duluth, Minnesota, and Akron, Ohio. These cards didn't say much, just, "I am here." He went back to Finland in 1913 to visit his mother, and, when he returned to this country, he came to Ashtabula because he had cousins there. He found work at the shipyards and then met my mother, Aino Glantz.

My mother was eighteen months old when she came to this country with her parents, in 1893. She went to the schools in Ashtabula Harbor, but didn't graduate from high school. The 1900 census states that her parents, her brother John (fourteen), and Aino (nine), spoke English, while the younger sisters, Sarah and Olga, did not. So that indicates that Finnish was mainly spoken in the home.

My father met my mother when she was a clerk in Kuivinen's Dry Goods Store. He lived nearby and met her when he shopped there. They were married in early 1915. My father worked in the shipyards and continued working there for forty-five years.

My dad favored the Finnish language, although he spoke English well enough at his workplace. But he always had an accent and used the common "Finglish" terms. Books, articles, and at least one dictionary have been written regarding the use of the "Finglish" terms by the early Finnish settlers in this country. I was a contributor to the American Finnish Dictionary.

I was their first child, born on November 6, 1915. I was named Tellervo, after the forest king's daughter in Finland's national epic, *Kalevala*. It means "Maiden of the Forest," but I'm better known as Tellie. My sister, Martha, was born next; then brother Robert; and Donna, the youngest girl.

Our home on Whitlam Street (West Fourteenth.) was almost new when we moved there in 1926 and large enough for our parents and four of us children. Before long, Father built a sauna, which was attached to the garage. It was the only sauna in the neighborhood of Finns and, needless to say, it was very popular. The men used the sauna first when it was hottest, and then the ladies went in. Coffee was always enjoyed after the sauna bath.

Our mother was a "happy homemaker" in the era when housekeeping was more arduous than it is today. She kept a regular schedule of doing laundry on Monday when a washboard was used and when clothes were boiled in a large copper boiler and then hung out to dry. Tuesday was ironing day. She was an especially fine cook who probably enjoyed baking the best. We remember her saying that she thought a bag of flour should be engraved on her tombstone. Canning and preserving foods was a necessity, and homemade soap was used in the sauna and for laundry. We wore homemade or altered clothes, and sometimes we wished we could have new ones bought from the store.

Both of our parents were friendly and outgoing and welcomed a variety of visitors, and a coffee table was always prepared for guests. There were church meetings, the PTA, and our teachers used to drop by after school for a cup of coffee. Sunday was church day and a special day to visit with other families. It was an era when a mother's place was in the home and fathers did their best to provide.

When there was a contagious disease in the home, the city nurse appeared to post a quarantine sign by the front door. We once had mumps and chickenpox cards posted at the same time, and I recall when all four of us were in a darkened room during a measles' epidemic.

We were exposed early to music when each of us had the privilege of taking some music lessons; some of us liked it better than others. Then we learned to listen when we played recordings on our early Victrola by McCormack, Heifetz, and Kreisler. On our first Atwater Kent radio, bought in the early 1930s, we listened to Saturday operas and Sunday symphony concerts. We enjoyed "Jack Benny" and "Rubinoff and His Violin" on Sunday evenings. Before long, our brother acquired amateur-radio equipment that he kept in his room. It may have been his inspiration when he later studied for his electrical engineering degree at Northeastern University in Boston.

Bob was the only one with a bicycle, and he rode it to school every day. We girls, however, always walked, and we all came home for lunch because it wasn't available in school. We graduated from Harbor High School, and it had the reputation of being a fine school. Today, it is remembered fondly by graduates. Earlier in this century [twentieth], about seventy-five percent of the students were of Finnish descent. During the Depression almost none of the students could afford to attend college, then in the 1940s the GI Bill afforded many servicemen and former servicemen the opportunity to attend. That's how my brother Bob was able to go.

There was one year during the Depression when our father was laid off. We weren't singled out, for nearly everyone we knew was in the same situation. When he returned to work as a night watchman, he received eighteen dollars a week. Ground meat sold for five cents a pound, and other groceries were comparable. Dad planted a large vegetable garden on an empty lot next door, and we didn't receive welfare as many others were forced to do, yet we were well aware that money and jobs were scarce.

We attended Sunday School each Sunday morning, and one of us was allowed to go to Sunday evening services with Mother at the Finnish Congregational Church. That was a privilege, even though the services then were in Finnish. Still, it was nice to walk alone with Mother and lean on her coat with the soft fur collar during the service. On Sunday nights coffee was served in the church dining room along with something sweet to eat. Children were given hot water with cream and sugar which was considered a special treat. Our Finnish Congregational Church was disbanded in 1958 and the building was demolished shortly after. I later attended services at the Second Congregational Church, and then joined Bethany Lutheran Church in 1991.

Our family holiday dinners were festive affairs, which we always shared. Our grandparents, aunts, and uncles lived across the street, and all food served was certainly of Finnish origin. One Thanksgiving Day we had to postpone dinner until evening because our cousin, Paul Glantz, played on the Harbor High football team against the arch rival, Ashtabula High, at the annual Thanksgiving Day game. We knew Santa Claus arrived on Christmas Eve soon after our aunt, Olga Glantz, arrived home from work at Carlisle's department store.

When I was fourteen, I tried to play a friend's violin. When my father noticed my interest, he ordered a violin for me from Montgomery Ward's catalog. I took lessons for a few years and then played in the school orchestra. My violin became a lifelong pastime, and I took additional lessons. I later went on a tour with the American Amateur Orchestra in 1968, and I became a founding member of the Ashtabula Area Orchestra and was its historian.

After my 1933 graduation from Harbor High, my first job was doing housework. Then I worked in an attorney's office. In 1936 I married William Lauri Raske. He was ten years older than I and worked in the shipyards. We had one daughter, Elaine, born in 1943.

My husband died unexpectedly on December 1, 1946, while he was sitting in the dentist's chair. It was a shock to become a widow and a single parent of a three-year-old daughter. I had to find work almost immediately. Beginning in 1947 I worked as a secretary at the Washington Elementary School, in the Jackson building, then at Harbor High School, where I also kept records for various student organizations. I married Raymond Sebell, a World War II veteran, in 1952, and he died in 1969. I continued working at the high school until 1972.

I belong to community organizations, too. I'm a member of the Ashtabula County Genealogy Society, the Finnish American Heritage Association, and Finlandia Foundation. I'm a forty-year member of the Colonial Club, and I also compiled and printed the "History of the Finnish Congregational Church." I enjoyed attending Finn Fests that are held in different American cities each year, and I'm a volunteer at the Ashtabula County Medical Center.

Tellie died in the Cleveland Clinic on April 28, 1998, at the age of eighty-two, survived by her daughter, Elaine Richardson; her sister, Donna Thorpe; and three grandchildren. A memorial service was held at Bethany Lutheran Church.

Amy Kaukonen Walsh

Amy's parents, Josef and Karoliina Kaukonen, were born in Ylistaro, Finland, in 1853 and 1855, respectively. They emigrated from Finland around 1889 with their first three daughters: Maria Alina, born in 1874; Aina Susanna, in 1876; and Ellen Matilda, 1883.

Amy Agnes was born May 2, 1891, in Elyria, Ohio. The only son, Armas Veikko, was born September 1, 1893, in Ashtabula Harbor.

The family apparently lived in Conneaut for some time. Because Amy graduated from Conneaut High School in 1910 with such high honors, she earned a scholarship to the Women's Medical College of Pennsylvania (Philadelphia). She then had a medical practice in Ashtabula for three years, but when three of her sisters' children died in infancy, she closed the practice and went to New York City, where she took postgraduate studies in children's diseases. During World War I she was a member of the Volunteer Medical Corps, U.S. Army.

In 1920 Amy resumed her medical practice in Fairport Harbor, Ohio, a Lake Erie port of nine thousand that included a large percentage of children.

In 1921 a committee approached Amy and asked her to run for mayor on the People's ticket. The committee believed men weren't exercising a strong enough hand in local government, especially since the Prohibition Amendment went into effect in 1920. Fairport citizens were outraged when a drunken police officer shot a fellow officer while at a bootlegger's resort. Because Amy was well-educated in the ill effects of bootleg liquor and wasn't timid about speaking out, the committee persisted and she finally agreed to run for office as a "dry candidate." She conducted her own campaign and promised to wage war on all whiskey runners and local bootleggers.

Because women were granted voting rights in 1920, we can imagine that many women turned out to vote that November day in 1921. The next day, the newspaper declared Amy the winner and announced it was the first time a woman in Fairport held such an important office. When it was discovered that she was the first woman in Ohio to hold a mayoral office, the newsmen began to hound her. Her youthful, pretty face began to appear in newspapers around the country and in magazines such as the *Ladies' Home Companion*. She was young, single, and attractive. Newsmen loved her; so, too, their readers, for she began to receive marriage proposals from near and afar. One New York man sent her a telegram saying that, if she didn't marry him, he would jump off the Brooklyn Bridge the following Tuesday. Amy telegraphed a terse reply: "Why wait until Tuesday?"

After taking office, she was confronted with a bundle of woes. Fairport citizens, along with most Americans, weren't yet taking prohibition laws seriously. With Canada a short sail across Lake Erie and Cleveland only thirty miles east, Fairport was a vulnerable location for bootleggers. Yet it was soon discovered that Amy would live up to her campaign promise of "cleaning up the town." She not only launched raids, but also participated with enthusiasm, even after receiving a black eye during a speakeasy raid. Another raid occurred on an undertaker's establishment when it was discovered he retrofitted a casket with a spigot to hold his cache of bootlegged whiskey. With the aid of village policeman, the casket-saloon was hoisted onto a truck, driven down the street, and the liquor dumped into Lake Erie. She assisted state marshals on additional raids.

As a medical doctor, Amy had the facilities to analyze confiscated liquor, such as raisin jack, and could truthfully proclaim: "It's not medicinal."

Newspaper reporters followed her diligently on every raid and during every court case she conducted. At first there was derisive laughter at the "girl mayoress," but she soon began to receive threatening letters, some containing death threats. These began shortly after she refused to grant licenses to soft-drink parlors that were found to violate prohibition laws. Although she proclaimed "these letters don't worry me," it was around this time that she acquired two large dogs that accompanied her everywhere.

Amy claimed to be the only woman physician of Finnish parentage in America, and on December 7, 1922, she attended the fifth-anniversary celebration of Finland's independence in New York City. At the Hotel Pennsylvania, she was asked to speak before a large gathering on the enforcement of the prohibition amendment. She admitted it was an experiment but reported it to be a success in her town, as there had been only two or three arrests in November when ordinarily there had been thirty.

During Amy's tenure as mayor, she received a large photograph of Warren G. Harding, who was then president of the United States. He penned this inscription below his photo: "To Dr. Amy Kaukonen, with high regard and good wishes to the first woman in Ohio to head the municipal government of her home city."

Despite her mayoral successes, Amy submitted a letter of resignation to the village council after serving nineteen months of her two-year term. The letter explained that she had received an unexpected and unusual offer that necessitated moving to another city. She was evasive with the press concerning her new opportunity, saying only that she had received an offer from Seattle, Washington, and felt that the position was one she wished to accept.

Amy next became the head of a women's hospital in Seattle, Washington. Here she met James L. Walsh, a pharmaceutical salesman from Boston, and they were married when both were in their forties. When Amy's mother became ill, the couple returned to Ohio to care for her. Karoliina Kaukonen died in 1942, at the age of eighty-seven. James Walsh died in 1971, and Amy lived independently in Painesville, Ohio, until she died in August 1984 at the age of ninety-three. The Walshes are buried in a Kaukonen family plot in Ashtabula's Edgewood Cemetery.

Ronald E. Korkate

All four of my grandparents emigrated from Finland. My father's parents were Henrik (Henry) Korkatti from Turku, Finland; and his wife, Iita (Ida), who was born in Raahe, Finland. They must have come here in the late 1880s or early 1890s because my uncle, Viktor Aleksander, was born in Ashtabula on

July 13, 1892; and my father, Hjalmar (Elmer), was born here on July 21, 1894. My aunt, Hulta Sofia, was also born here on August 20, 1898. I'm not sure when, but their last name was anglicized to Korkate instead of Korkatti.

My mother's parents were John and Elizabeth (Halperi) Kuula. They emigrated from Lapua, Finland, and went first to northern Wisconsin. My mother, Tyyne Kuula, was born in Iron Belt, Wisconsin, on December 28, 1906. I'm not sure when her family moved to Ashtabula, but, according to Bethany Lutheran Church records, she was confirmed there on June 18, 1922. All my grandparents were members of the first Bethany Lutheran Church, and my parents were married on June 5, 1929, by Pastor Joki.

My dad worked for the New York Central Railroad, but my mother, who was called "Tibbie," didn't work out of the home until my dad died, then she worked at the Madison Restaurant, which was on Morton Drive at that time. I had one sister, Marilyn (Ovak), who was born in 1932, but she died in 1996.

Marilyn and I both went to Washington Elementary School and Harbor High School. I graduated from Harbor High in 1948. I remember going to family picnics and reunions at Lake Shore Park and having a good time there when I was a youngster.

Both of my grandfathers also worked for the New York Central Railroad, but both of them had died before I was born. I remember both grandmothers, though. They used to have coffee brewing all the time, and they made *nisua* [cardamom-flavored coffee bread] and *hapenleipä* [sour rye bread]. I started going to the sauna, too, when I was a young child. My grandmother Kuula had a sauna on West Sixth Street, and I used to go there with my parents. After she died, we went to the public sauna on West Eighth Street. I remember playing basketball in Sovinto Hall when I was a kid, but I don't know much about the other halls and beaches that my mother talked about.

I used to go swimming with my friends, and we'd play ball and other games. In winter we'd go sled riding and skating. I had a pair of skis, but didn't get to use them much around Ashtabula. And I liked to go down to the docks and watch those huge cranes lift up a railroad car and turn it over to dump coal into a pile. There's not as much activity on the docks now. When my dad worked for the railroad, we'd get annual passes to take trips to Canada, Cleveland, or Erie. I really enjoyed those trips.

My grandmother Kuula had a barn behind her house on lower West Sixth Street, and sometimes raised chickens or a calf. She raised a calf for the beef, and I remember when they butchered it. She drained the blood for blood pudding that she molded into the shape of a cow before she baked it. She had a sauna that she charged admission for, and she sold homemade beer for ten cents a bottle. I went there as a kid and shook some bottles until the corks blew. She got mad at me, but then she couldn't help laughing. After my grandfather died, she rented out the second-floor apartment in her house, and she made rugs on her rug loom and sold them. Her father had made the rug loom back in the 1890s.

[Shortly after his 1996 interview, Ronald donated his grandmother's rug loom to the FAHA.]

My father was off work for a while during the Depression, but I don't remember specifically how hard times were. I can remember, though, when I was only four or five years old, when my father and a couple of neighbors made home-brewed beer and bottled it in the basement. I was in high school during World War II and too young to get drafted, but I had relatives who served in the war.

A first cousin of my mother's was Gus Hall who ran for president on the Communist ticket during the 1950s. My mother told us not to say anything about him to anyone. She was deathly afraid the FBI would come knocking on the door to ask her about her association with a Communist. She saw Gus in a restaurant once in Cleveland. He just looked at her and didn't say anything, and she didn't say anything, either.

After high school, I went to Youngstown. I met my wife when we were both enrolled in the Youngstown Hospital School of Nursing. We both graduated from there in 1955, then Rhoda (Warg) and I were married on February 18, 1956. We first lived in Ashtabula, then moved to Youngstown for ten years. We then lived in Lima for over twenty years. In 1987 we came back to Ashtabula for nine years. When we were in Ashtabula, I sang in Bethany Lutheran's Chancel Choir and in the Town Choir. John Riddell was the one who invited me to join the Masonic Lodge. Then we moved once more, back to Lima.

We have two sons, Matthew and Richard. We liked to take the boys on train rides, like I used to do. We took a trip once to Washington from Youngstown and ate in the dining car. That's one thing I miss—the trains.

Ron Korkate retired after thirty years as director of nursing at Oakwood Forensic Center, Lima. He was a member of St. Marks United Methodist Church, a member of the Allen County Senior Citizens, and belonged to the Masonic Lodge in Ashtabula.

Ron died in Lima's St. Rita's Medical Center on January 31, 2005. He was seventy-four. Survivors include his wife, two sons, five grandchildren, and three great-grandchildren. He is buried in Greenlawn Memory Gardens, North Kingsville, Ohio.

Kaarlo Johannes (John) Karbacka

My mother's name was Maria Justiina Sippola, and she was born in Ylistaro, Finland. She immigrated to America during the 1890s. My father, Jakob Karpakka, was born in Isokyro. He was naturalized on April 4, 1898, but I think he came over several years before that. I still have my father's passport and his naturalization paper. Our last name is spelled Karpakka on his paper, but sometime over the years it was changed to Karbacka. Both families settled in Ashtabula Harbor because they knew other Finns there and work was available.

My folks didn't meet in Finland. They met in Ashtabula and were married there. They lived for a while on Bridge Street, and then they moved to Tivision Street, and the last place I remember them having was on Cherry Street, which is now West Ninth. They never bought their own home.

My father worked for thirty years at the Hanna Docks—the old docks, when it was up the river from the lift bridge. He was a shoveler, of which they had many, because the way the ships were unloaded. It was all with pick and shovel. Then when the new docks were built on the lakefront, they employed fewer men, because of mechanization.

During World War I, there were lots of jobs in the shipyards of the Seattle area, so my family moved there since the dock work had gotten slow. I had two older brothers by that time, Martin and William. But by the time they got there, the war had ended, so my dad had to work in the coal mines in Burnett, Washington, and Burnett is where I was born, on January 25, 1919. During the time my dad was working in the mines, my uncle, John Sippola, worked on a different shift, and he was killed in a mine explosion. My mother said, "That's it; no more mining!"

So we came back to Ashtabula and my brothers and I went to Washington Elementary School and Harbor High School. Our family belonged to Bethany Lutheran Church.

My mother baked *nisua* once a week, and other Finnish breads; and of course she made *mojakka* [stew] and *riisipuuro* [rice pudding] served with strawberries.

I remember Sovinto Hall, which started out as a temperance place, and they used to have social gatherings there and Humina Band concerts. They had plays on the stage, and they used to have basketball games on the weekends.

I never played, just horsed around. They also had dances, and the annual ball on New Year's Eve was a big, big thing. In fact, Les Brown's Band was booked to come there one time, but he sent a telegram and said he was snowed in—in Minnesota—so he couldn't make it. They wound up getting a band from Cleveland. We used to go to the Modern Woodmen picnic grounds where they had all-day affairs, especially on Sunday. We would play games and have lots to eat, traditional Finnish foods, of course.

We used to go swimming when we were kids down at the number eleven slip, where they used to have the coal dock. During summer vacation I would be down there all day, and every day, and I always brought a lunch with me. That's when I got too much sunshine, because we would swim naked. I'm paying for it now by having cancer removed from my skin in various places.

The Depression was kind of rough going for everybody. My father died at the beginning of the Depression in 1930, and there was no such thing as food stamps or welfare as we know today. That's why I went to work at an early age. At the age of twelve, my first job was at the Orange-Crush Bottling Works, and my pay was to take home a quart bottle or two of soda pop at the end of the week. Then I was taking a case of pop home, and then it got to be that I was getting paid for it. I was actually getting paid a wage each week. Ed Broughton bought the bottling works and it became the NeHi Bottling Works. I worked there all summer long and evenings and weekends during the winter. In 1936 I was being paid six dollars a week during the summer, and I asked him for a raise. He said he couldn't afford it, so then I told him I was going to ship out on the Great Lakes. He told me I was too young and that I'd never be able to, but I thought I would, anyway. I used to go and meet each boat as they came in to see if there was anyone quitting, and I finally got on one.

I was seventeen [1936] when I first shipped out, but first they let me go back home to get my clothes and my shipping book. I bought a few things on the way home, on credit, and also bought a suitcase. It was about two A.M. and my mother was sleeping, but I guess I made some noise with the dresser drawers because she came in and asked me what I was doing. When I told her I was shipping out, she said, "No, you're not! You're too young!" And she started throwing the clothes out of the suitcase almost as fast as I could get them in there. But I finally won out, and she gave in, but she was brokenhearted. My two brothers were already sailing on the lakes.

One day I let her know I was going to be coming in to the number nine coal dock for a load of coal and I would walk down to the docks to meet her. This was in October—a nice day—and when she saw them load me on the bo'sun [boatswain] chair and swing me out, she started to cry. There I was on the bo'sun chair with nothing but a piece of rope between me and the dock. It had been quite a while since I had been there, so they let me go home for a while. I sailed thirteen years after that and became a mate.

In the old days, when I got out of school, a young person could always find work, but now there is a lack of good-paying jobs here for young people.

I married Elizabeth (Betty) Hendrickson in September of 1940. Betty was born in Sweden and came to this country when she was five years old. When our son, Raymond, was born in 1943, I had been inducted into the coast guard as a lieutenant. After the war I went back on the lakes. I had my stationary engineer's license, so one winter Mr. Wenner came down to the shipyard and asked me if I would take the fireman's job at the Harbor High School because their fireman was retiring. So I took the fireman's job during winters and went back to sailing in the spring. I was at the high school for three winters. Our daughter, Shareen, was born in 1947, and I quit sailing in 1948 so I wouldn't be gone so much. And my back went haywire from shoveling coal by hand, so I gave up and went into carpentry work.

We first rented a house on West Third Street. Then, after a couple years of renting, they asked us if we wanted to buy the house, so we did and lived there for eighteen years until we built the house on Norman Avenue. My mother lived with us on West Third for several years, and then she decided she would try living by herself. And she did, on Oak and Cherry Street. She died in 1961.

The new house took me three and a half years to build because I was working forty hours a week in the carpenter shop at Laird Lumber. I started building our house in 1957, working evenings and weekends, and we finally moved there in 1960.

I worked in carpentry until 1969, then I was hired as Ashtabula City building inspector; I stayed there for fifteen years before I retired.

In 1989 we went to visit our relatives. We first went to Kalmar, Sweden, where my wife was born, and met her cousins, and then went to Stockholm, where her first cousin was the fire chief. We also spent time with my Finnish relatives in Ylistaro and Isokyro. We hope to go back some day.

We have six grandchildren. Ray recently retired from Rockwell Standard in Fairview, Iowa, and has four children. His wife is head nurse in a hospital there. Shareen got her teaching degree at Kent State, then went into interior design. She is now a substitute teacher along with her design work. Her husband, John Linton, is head psychologist at the Charleston Medical

Center, and is a university professor. They live in Charleston, West Virginia, and have two children. We spent our winters in Florida for the past twenty years, but we now [2006] live full time in Ashtabula and just make brief trips to Charleston or points south.

Impi Julia Maenpaa Kontas

My father, Mikko Maenpaa, and his brother Matti were born in Sweden, near the Finnish border. Their last name first became Bauch because my great-grandfather, who was a Swedish sea captain, landed in Germany and married a German woman whose name was Bauch so he had to take her name. They said she was a midwife and town nurse and that she lived to be 104. But when Mikko and Matti's mother died, their father married a Finnish woman and moved to her place in Särvijoki, Finland. Then they had to take her name—Maenpaa. My father and his brother didn't like it at all when they had to move and take her name, but they had to. It was a tradition, or it was the law, but that's how we got the name Maenpaa.

My mother's name was Liisa Perskari. I don't know where she met my father, but they were married in Finland and lived on a small farm in Laihia, near Vaasa. I have pictures from their marriage. My mother went to school and was more educated than my father, so she taught him to read and spell and figure math. My oldest sister, Lempi, was born in 1895, and then, after a few years, my father went to America by himself, around 1897. He worked there for a while, then went back to Finland for my mother and Lempi. But my aunt wouldn't let them take Lempi because she said they didn't have a home for her.

So my dad and mother came here in third class and everybody was packed in like sardines on top of one another. But everyone was congenial and they arrived to Ellis Island okay. I don't know why they came to Ashtabula, but I suppose because there was a lot of Finnish people here and the docks were here. It must have been around 1901 or 1902 when they all came, because my sister Saima [Kotila] was born in 1903. I was born on May 13, 1904, when they lived on Morton Drive.

The first house my dad bought was on Hulbert Avenue—on top of the hill. It was an eight-room house, four rooms down and four rooms up. No, it's not still there, but that's where I was raised. My father was a boilermaker at McKinnon Iron Works for many years, and had to go on the boats sometimes to fix their boilers. In 1906 my father went back to Finland and brought my sister Lempi back with him. By that time, she was eleven years old, and the first time she saw her younger sisters.

I didn't go to Washington School because there were so many children that my first grade was in the Methodist Church on Lake Avenue. My second grade was in a house in back of West Third Street because there was no room for everybody in the regular schools. Lots of kids those days. Usually every family had a kid in every grade. I went to Harbor High School, and I was a forward when we played basketball because I was so tall. But I didn't graduate until the summer after. I didn't have enough credits for English, so I had to take English the following summer to get through.

Our church was Bethany Lutheran. My father was great for celebrating birthdays and anniversaries, and we always went on picnics and my mother was always the cook. She was always cooking. She baked *nisua* and bread because we always had two boarders. We all got along in four rooms. If they came from Finland, and they knew my folks, they would come over and stay until they got married. Mother made a lot of meat and potatoes, and our favorite thing was when she cooked raisins, prunes, and other fruits together. We called it "love soup." My mother made rugs on a loom, too. Her brother, Matt Perskari, made the loom. Then later on, when she quit making rugs, she gave the loom to me.

Sovinto Hall was where we used to keep our Christmas. Everybody who belonged to the association had their Christmas or Christmas Eve upstairs in the hall. There was a great big Christmas tree, and everybody wrapped their toys there for their children. It was Depression time, so you didn't have to have a Christmas tree at your home. Everybody enjoyed it at the hall. They had a program, and then they always had coffee and other stuff to go with it. The Humina Band used to entertain at all kinds of picnics and social affairs. Their ladies, or wives, held coffee socials to buy new uniforms for the band before they traveled to Finland in 1927.

They had plays at Sovinto. My sister and I and lots of friends our age were gypsies in *Hevospaimen*. My father was in it and my oldest sister was in it. That was in 1914.

We used to go to Rennick's Meat Market. My mother couldn't speak English but got along because she pointed to the things that she wanted. We went to the Finnish Bakery on West Eighth Street. I remember Sippola's bakery. There was Fannie and Jenny and Alice and a real good-looking brother. We lived in back of them and we went across lots to the stores.

We played hopscotch and jacks, and we played hide-and-seek when it got dark. We went swimming all summer long. We would get poison ivy and be white with calamine lotion on. Everybody looked alike and nobody cared. In the winter we went sledding, and, right by the river, by the bridge, they'd build a bonfire and we'd roast marshmallows. We used to take rides on the old swing bridge. When it came in we'd jump on it for a few seconds, just for a ride, then jump off again. But finally they stopped us because one kid fell. He didn't catch the bridge and fell on the pilings, but he didn't get hurt bad, and he didn't fall in the water.

My first job was working at Geneva-on-the-Lake. I was a short-order cook and I made hamburgers and hot dogs.

I was married the first time to Ray St. John, and we had a daughter, Geraldine, who was born in 1923. We were married fifteen years, then I was a widow for eight years, and then I married Vaino Kontas in 1944. He was in the service, so I worked at the Fork and Hoe ordinance plant where we made bayonets during World War II. Their own bus took us from the Harbor to the plant uptown.

Impi Kontas died in the Ashtabula County Medical Center on June 15, 2000, at the age of ninety-six. She was survived by her daughter, one grandson, and two great-grandsons.

Aini (Anna) Elviira Sippola Owen

Anna's father, Isaak Sippola, was born on September 15, 1866, in Nurmo, Finland. He was the sixth child of eight born to Johan and Sanna (Antintytar) Salomon. Anna's mother, Kaisa (Katherine) Malkamaki, was born in Nurmo, Finland, in 1873, one of six children. Isaak and Kaisa were married on March 13, 1896, and both applied for a five-year passport to America in April 1896. The Sippola surname appeared on this application, an indication that Isaak worked last on a Sippola farm. At that time, a man adopted the surname of the landowner. Their first child, Johan Kustaa (John Charles), was born in Nurmo on January 1, 1897, after Isaak had already immigrated to the United States.

Isaak worked first in Vermont as a stonecutter before moving on to Fairport Harbor, Ohio, then to Ashtabula, and finally to Conneaut, where he settled and found work before sending for Kaisa's passage. Kaisa and baby John apparently arrived in late 1897, or early 1898, for their second child, Sanna Liisa (Elizabeth) was born on October 22, 1898.

During the following sixteen years, eleven more children were born to the couple: Olga Maria (Mary) in 1899; Jenny Katariina, 1901; Hilda Loviisa, 1903; Iisakki (Isaac/Ike) Nikolai, 1904; Senia (Virginia) Sophia, 1906; Iita (Ida) Eliina, 1908; Lempi (Leona) Matilta, 1910; Fanni Martta (Martha) and Saima Sylvia (twins), 1911; Aini (Anna) Elviira, June 30, 1913; and Emmi Laina, 1915. Emmi, the youngest, was born retarded and an epileptic. She was cared for at home until she died at the age of thirty-five. With so many growing girls, they slept crosswise, five to a bed. The two boys slept in a separate unheated building where snow often sifted through the cracks of the walls on windy, snowy winter nights and settled on their pillows.

Anna remembered the deadly tornado that struck Lorain, Ohio, on June 28, 1924, when she was eleven. The high winds moved eastward from Lorain along the Lake Erie shoreline toward Conneaut, slackening somewhat as they went along. Anna was outside when she saw the blackened sky and felt the roaring wind. She attempted to run to the house but later found herself, dazed, blown into the cornfield.

Anna played center position in high-school basketball games as she was five feet, ten inches tall. She was the only one in her family to graduate from high school, because her older sisters quit school and went to work. Many of them went to Cleveland, working as domestics. Once, while visiting her sister Elizabeth (Olson) in Cleveland, a knock was heard and Anna went to answer the door. There stood two men who had come to move a piano to the second floor of this apartment building. One of the men, Samuel Owen, would become Anna's future husband. Sam and his brother had come to Cleveland from Florida. They owned a moving company at the time Sam met Anna. Anna and Sam were married on February 10, 1934, when Anna was twenty-one.

Anna had always had menstrual problems, and a doctor told her that the problem would cease after she had children. Such was not the case, however, for when Raymond Clifford, her only child, was born on January 21, 1935, her heavy menstruations resumed to the point that she would require hospitalization. The only remedy at that time was a hysterectomy. Anna required a blood transfusion before surgery, and her brother, Ike, was found to have the matching blood type. As they lay side by side during the direct transfusion, he tried to humor her by telling her that she would now have a craving for Copenhagen snuff, the brand he chewed.

Unfortunately, the surgeon left a portion of one ovary to provide her with some estrogen because there was no artificial substitute at the time. The consequences of that decision would adversely affect her later on.

Sam and Anna built their home in Amherst, Ohio, and Sam owned a garage, mainly for wheel aligning. Anna did bookkeeping for the business while Raymond was growing up. She recalled how delighted she was each payday when Sam bought one sheet of drywall to install in their house that was being built piece by piece while living in it.

On October 4, 1957, Sam was stricken with a sudden heart attack and died at the age of forty-nine. He had told Anna to keep their pink Cadillac and learn to drive so, at forty-four, Anna followed his instructions and learned to drive a car. Raymond married Silvia Bateman on November 4, 1957, and, after living with Anna for a time, they moved to a farm near Albion, Pennsylvania.

When Anna was fifty, she married George Septaric and moved into his house in Lorain after selling her Amherst house. Four years later, in 1967, she was diagnosed with ovarian cancer and was given radiation treatments. Her health was stable for a while, then in early 1975 Anna was again diagnosed with cancer, and this time underwent chemotherapy. In 1976 she and George were divorced under amicable conditions. He continued her hospitalization and gave her his old car whenever he bought a new one.

Anna moved to Ashtabula into the Gulfview Apartments in 1980, where she was nearer her remaining two sisters, Ida and Martha, and to her son's family. By then she also had three grandsons: Samuel, born in 1960; Daniel, 1962; and Kirk, 1976. In addition, since her parents had twenty-nine grandchildren and fifty-nine great-grandchildren, there were many nieces and nephews to visit at reunions and other family gatherings. If there were a few present who did not know her, she waved her arm around and said, "I'm everyone's aunt Ann."

When cancer struck yet a third time, Anna was admitted to the Cleveland Clinic, where additional chemotherapy treatments were planned. After the first series, she suffered so many side effects that she refused to continue and came home. Between her cancer bouts, Anna maintained a positive attitude and enjoyed life. She went dancing with several lady friends, and always kept a well-groomed appearance. She enjoyed jokes and stories and was rarely without a laugh or smile. Because her income was limited to her Social Security, she began sewing and selling clown dolls. She took orders, then designed clown dolls with appropriate costumes for every holiday, for graduations, and birthdays.

In 1988 Anna required hip-replacement surgery. While undergoing preoperative tests, she was instructed to see a urologist, who diagnosed a blocked ureter. She was transferred to the Cleveland Clinic once again. At the clinic a cystostomy was performed wherein a tube was attached from one kidney down into an exterior plastic bag. The problem wasn't with the kidney, but with the ureter that had been damaged by the radiation received years before. Before long, the same procedure was required on the remaining kidney. The hip-replacement surgery had been successful, but it was believed that the radiation had had a drastic effect on her bones, because her height was reduced over the years from five-foot-ten inches to five-foot-four. Her teeth were also affected and began loosening, so she was subsequently fitted with dentures. Her weight fell to 105 pounds. In May 1989 one more surgery was necessitated by a colon blockage. Her intestines and colon had been hardened by the radiation, and cancerous tumors were intertwined so that it was impossible to remove all of the cancer; consequently, she was fitted with a colostomy bag. When she went home after three weeks, she quipped that she had, like the nursery rhyme, "three bags full." With the help of home health nurses, delivery of Meals on Wheels, and assistance from her daughter-in-law and several nieces, she was able to remain in her apartment. Occasional hospital stays were required whenever she became dehydrated or if one of the stomas (appliance connecting tubes to the body) needed replacement. In 1991 a second hip-replacement was performed that left her practically immobile.

On June 30, 1993, Anna celebrated her eightieth birthday in the community room of her apartment building with nieces, nephews, and her daughter-in-law present. She requested strawberry shortcake to be served rather than a birthday cake, and she smiled brightly for photos, seated in a wheelchair. She continued to remain cheerful, maintaining interest in her family, favorite TV programs, and the world news. She had a telephone and a TV remote by her side, with a bedside table for water and snacks. Home health services continued.

By 1993 Anna had outlived all her siblings, with only two sisters and her mother reaching eighty. Her father died of a heart attack, at age sixty-nine, on the night following his fortieth wedding anniversary celebration in 1936. Her mother had a stroke when she was seventy-five, which left her bedridden, and her daughters took turns caring for her in her home. One week there seemed to be no one available who could stay with her, and one daughter, Leona, said, "Mother, you should have had more children!" Her mother died in June of 1953 at the age of eighty.

Anna's valiant battle with cancer had stretched, off and on, over a period of twenty-six years. She used to remark that she had cancer every eight years, as though she were talking about the common cold.

Anna died peacefully with her son, grandson, and daughter-in-law at her side on August 15, 1993, and is buried in Center Cemetery, Conneaut, Ohio, in a Sippola family plot.

These accounts of Anna Owen's life were written by her niece, N. Fairburn, who often drove her to the Cleveland Clinic for tests or treatment. Information about her parents' emigration was provided by Linda Riddell.

Jerry Mervin (Haksluoto) Peterson

My paternal grandparents, Alexander and Sofia (Ylitalo) Haksluto, were born in Finland in 1876 and 1881, respectively. They immigrated to the United States and settled in Ashtabula Harbor, around 1898. My grandfather Haksluoto worked as an oiler for machinery at the docks. They had nine children: Lempi, Helen, Jerry (my father), Pearl, Arne, Hazel, Arthur, Betty, and Paul.

My maternal grandfather, Jacob Peltoma, was born on August 11, 1881, in Laihia, Finland, and my maternal grandmother, Ida Somppi, was born on December 21, 1874, in Ylistaro, Finland. They emigrated from Finland and settled in Fairport Harbor. This village is thirty miles west of Ashtabula, on Lake Erie's shore. They had a large family of twelve children: Aliina, John, Theodore, Swanters, Neil, Martha (my mother), Martin, Hilmer, Esther, Ina, Carl, and William.

My father, Jerry Arvo Haksluoto, was born in Ashtabula in 1903. My mother, Martha Elisa Peltoma, was born on September 5, 1905, in Fairport Harbor. My parents met and were married in Fairport and had four children: Jerry (I was the oldest), Elaine, Wayne, and Doris. I was born November 3, 1925. At that time my father worked as a boilermaker for the Fairport-Painesville & Eastern Railroad. That was a railroad line that served the Diamond-Alkali chemical plant in Fairport.

When I was three years old my grandfather Haksluoto died at age fifty-two in 1928. He worked at the Pittsburgh and Lake Erie ore docks, and someone accidentally dropped a heavy object from above that struck and killed him.

I remember the Depression years very well. During those years the schools sent census takers door to door for enrollment purposes. They discovered that among four thousand residents, fifty percent were Finnish, forty-nine percent were Hungarian, and one percent Slovenian. Most of the men worked at the ore docks or at the Diamond-Alkali plant, and they all had their working hours reduced. Then families had to charge their groceries at neighborhood stores until they received some wages. People were more trustworthy in those days, even during hard times. Housewives had to shop for meat and fresh vegetables daily as very few had refrigerators in their homes. Iceboxes were used for summer food storage and outdoor window boxes were attached for use during winter months. Grocery stores were referred to as "neighborhood refrigerators." Since almost everyone was poor, youngsters had to be inventive. For instance, I remember how we boys made our own scooters from wooden orange crates. We would attach a crate to old roller skate wheels, and then make a handle out of a piece of sawed-off wood.

Entertainment didn't cost much during those times. I can remember when a piece of candy or a stick of gum could be purchased for a penny. An ice-cream cone was a nickel. It was only ten cents for a Saturday afternoon double-feature at our Lyric movie theater, and five cents bought a bag of popcorn. Wednesday was family night when admission for an entire family was just twenty-five cents. Then between double features they would raffle off food baskets that had been donated by local grocery-store owners. It was a real bonus to win one of those.

One day my dad came home and announced to us that from now on our surname would be Peterson instead of Haksluoto. I don't believe he had it taken care of legally, but we've been Peterson ever since, and it sure is easier for others to pronounce and spell.

My greatest tragedy, while growing up, was the day my dad died. Just like his father, it was an accident at work. He drowned in the Grand River, and he was only thirty-seven. This was in 1940, so my mother became a widow at age thirty-five, and had four young children to support. So she had to go to work at the local Industrial Rayon Corporation. She never owned or drove a car, so she traveled to work by bus. Mother worked in several different places throughout the years; in fact, she didn't retire from her school crossing guard's job until she was seventy-five.

My father had a $1,000 life insurance policy, but, since his was an accidental death, my mother received an additional $1,000. The four-room house we had been renting for sixteen dollars a month came up for sale for $2,400. My mother wanted to buy it, as the landlord had said he'd sell it to her for $2,000. Now three of her brothers were all in building trades: one was an electrician, one was a carpenter, and one a painter and rigger. All three of them advised her against buying the house, saying it wasn't worth that much. But she told her brothers that she had to keep a roof over her kids' heads and she went ahead and bought it.

When someone asked my mother, in later years, why she never remarried, she said she didn't want anyone else bossing her kids. Then when the kids were grown and on their own, she said marriage no longer interested her. When Mother died in 1988, her house sold for $48,000, so I guess she made a wise decision, after all.

When my dad died, I was fourteen and the others were twelve, nine, and six. In order to help my mother I worked as a janitor's helper for three hours a day at the high school—one hour before school and two hours after school. I earned twenty-five cents an hour, but even that helped our family. I kept up this same routine for the next three years.

After my 1943 graduation from Fairport Harding High School, I worked as a laborer at the Diamond-Alkali plant. Then in January 1944 I joined the navy. I wasn't called for overseas' duty, but served instead at the Brooklyn Navy Yard. I was discharged as a pharmacist's mate, third-class, in March of 1946. The GI Bill that Congress passed in 1944 enabled me to enroll at Ohio's Kent State University. I received my bachelor's degree in education in 1950 and was then certified to teach secondary social studies as well as elementary education.

I married a hometown Fairport girl, Alberta E. Stuuri, in March 1950. She was born on November 21, 1927, and was a 1946 graduate of Harding High. Her grandfather, William Hervey, was well known as a very strict supervisor at the ore docks.

Alberta and I moved to Ashtabula in the summer of 1950 as I had been hired as principal of the North Kingsville Elementary School, and I also taught eighth-grade classes. North Kingsville School became part of the Ashtabula-Edgewood District in 1956 and, beginning in 1962, after Ashtabula County schools became consolidated, the Edgewood District was thereafter known as the Buckeye Local School District.

Alberta received a college degree by taking courses over the years, yet she preferred to stay at home after we had our three daughters: Elizabeth (Johnson), was born in 1954; Gretchen (Friend), in 1961; and Laurel (Flautt), in 1963.

I worked to obtain my master's degree in education from Columbia University's Teachers' College in New York City from 1950 through 1956. I took courses at Columbia during five summers and, since we were always a close family, my wife and daughters went along, and we stayed in rented apartments. Then a series of promotions followed: I became director of curriculum (K–12) from 1967 to 1973. Then from 1967 to 1971, I returned to Columbia and was awarded a second Master of Arts degree as well as receiving a superintendent's certificate. I was then qualified to serve as superintendent of Buckeye Local Schools (1973–85). I retired as superintendent in 1985, and then served as a consultant to the Ashtabula County Board of Education from 1986 to 1988. In July 1988, the board hired me to serve as interim superintendent of Jefferson Area Schools for three months; instead, that position resulted in a three-year term.

I thought I was beginning my retirement years on January 1, 1991, yet such wasn't the case. Fairport Harbor Schools, in my hometown, needed a superintendent as their present superintendent's contract wasn't renewed. Alberta was a cancer patient at that time, yet she encouraged me to accept the temporary, three-month position. But again, that position turned into a three-year term. During my tenure in Fairport, the citizens passed an operating levy and a permanent improvement levy.

Alberta passed away on August 5, 1995, and so wasn't able to join me in my retirement years, which officially began in July of 1998. I'm currently [2005] serving my last year of a four-year term as a member of the Buckeye Local Board of Education. So after a forty-two-year career in education, I believe it's been a positive experience and a memorable one. Yet I don't believe I could have done it without the encouragement of my family, colleagues, and friends, who seemed to instill in me the necessary confidence.

I've also been a member of Ashtabula's Messiah Lutheran Church for more than fifty years, and my future plans include continuing my membership. I'm glad I have more time now to spend with my family and my fiancée, Dora (Turano) Ferritto. I'm the father of three girls, but they made me a grandfather of five boys: Matthew, Alexander, Jacob, Jerry, and Andrew.

Martha Viena Jarvi Ranta

My father, John Jarvi, was born in Ylistaro, Finland, in 1879. When he was nineteen, in 1898, he immigrated to the United States and went to Montana for two years. Then he went to Conneaut, where his father, Jacob Jarvi, had settled. My grandfather Jarvi passed away before I was born and is buried in Conneaut City Cemetery.

My mother's name was Hilma Fredriika Orvasaari. She emigrated from Kauhava with her parents and they also settled in Conneaut. My parents met in Conneaut and were married there in the old Finnish Lutheran Church.

My dad and my mother first lived on Day Street, then they bought the house on Dean Avenue, about 1915, and that's where most of us were born. My dad was a foreman of boat repairs at the Pittsburgh and Conneaut Dock Company. There were people who cursed us because my father was able to keep working during the Depression. He retired from the docks in 1949, when he was seventy years old.

My two brothers were Mauno and Jack Jarvi, and my sister's name was Helmi, but she changed it to Pearl; her married name was Peura. Since Jarvi means lake in Finnish, my brother Jack later changed his name to Jack Lake, but he was the only one who changed his name.

I was born on April 18, 1907. We went to the Dean Avenue School, right at the end of our street. My father was very active in the Lutheran church; in fact, he was president of the church council for almost eighteen years.

We used to go to Kilpi Hall, especially for the band concerts. My dad first played the cornet for more than twenty-five years, then he later played a French horn in the Pohjan Alto [Northern Wave] Band. My brother, Mauno, started playing with this band in 1920, when he was ten; he first played the piccolo, then the flute. Mauno could play the accordion, saxophone, and cornet, too. Mauno started directing the band in 1950, then in 1954 the band was known as the Conneaut Harbor Band. They used to play for parades and concerts and all kinds of celebrations. My dad played with this band for fifty-four years.

On Sunday afternoons our home was always open for youngsters. We'd play the piano and sing. I think we had one of the first radios in Conneaut Harbor. During the baseball season we'd open the dining room window and youngsters would sit around on the lawn and listen to the games. Later, we had a bigger radio with a mammoth horn. We were listening to that one day in 1924, I think it was, when all of a sudden the dining-room chandelier start shaking and we thought it was an earthquake, but then we heard that a tornado blew through Conneaut. We all were frightened; everything was so spooky.

I remember *Juhannus* when my grandmother, Maria Heino, who lived with us, would decorate the porch with different wildflowers. Then she would serve coffee there for her friends. On Christmas we went to early church at six A.M., and then came home for our breakfast and to open our gifts. We had a hill just a block behind us—Garden Street Hill—where kids went skiing and sledding. Mother would go with us and we'd go down the hill with a cardboard box.

After my 1925 graduation from Conneaut High School, my first job was with a Glidden Paint store in Cleveland. During World War II, I worked for State Auto Insurance in Cleveland, and then they transferred me to their Detroit office. I met my husband, Jacob Richard (Dick) Ranta when I was living in Detroit. He was born in Isokyro, Finland, and had immigrated to Ashtabula with his parents when he was six years old. Their name had been Skarb in Swedish, but Dick's uncle changed it to Ranta when he was in the army, so the other brothers changed their last names, too.

Dick had worked in a New York City bank as a bookkeeper, and in Detroit he worked at the Harbor Bank. In later years, he got his CPA from Detroit University, then he became a cost accountant for Murray Corporation. I also worked in the accounting field as a statistical secretary.

We have one son, John Richard, (Rick) who was born in Detroit, October 2, 1947. Dick died in 1962, and Rick and I then moved to Ashtabula. Rick and Barbara were married in 1974 and have four children: Allison, Jacob, William, and Laura. We all are members of Bethany Lutheran Church.

Martha's later years were spent in an apartment in Ashtabula Towers. She died at the Ashtabula County Nursing Home on August 29, 1998, at the age of ninety-one.

Mauno Johannes (John) Laituri

My father, Antti Laituri, emigrated from Harma, Finland, when he was a young man. This was during the late 1890s, and he settled in Conneaut, Ohio. He found work there as a crane operator at the Pittsburgh and Conneaut Dock Company.

My mother, Maria Toppari, emigrated from Huhmarkoski, which is near Kauhava. She worked as a domestic in Conneaut. My folks met in Conneaut and were married there in 1901. They first lived in East Conneaut in a house that overlooked Lake Erie. My oldest brother, Martin, was born in 1903; then the second one, Mauno, died from pneumonia when he was two. But eight more kids followed, and all our names began with the letter M: Martha, Matthew, Milma, Mickey, Mauri, Marie, Mauno Johannes (me), and then Melvin, the youngest.

They named me Mauno Johannes, the same name as the boy who died, but I went by John in school, and the family always called me Jussie, which is pronounced "Yussie" in Finnish. And sometimes they just shortened this to "Yuss." I was born in 1921 in Ashtabula, the same year my oldest brother graduated from Harbor High School. Around 1918, our family moved from Conneaut to Ashtabula, where my dad got a job in the shipyards. Then when World War I ended, so did Dad's job. He had several jobs that lasted only a short time, so then he finally went to Detroit where my older brothers were working.

I went to the Harbor Special Schools, and when I was in the fifth grade, me and some of my friends were rough-housing around at recess. One friend said that, boy, his heart was really beating fast. So I felt the left side of my chest and I couldn't feel any heartbeat. Then I moved my hand to the right side, and then I could feel a heartbeat. So I told my friend this, and he just laughed at me. When I told my teacher, and then told my family later, no one paid any attention to what I said and just brushed me off. But when I was in the sixth grade, all the kids were given a physical exam, and the doctor found my heart was positioned on the right, so I was glad someone finally believed me.

During the Depression years we had a big vegetable garden, and we stored potatoes in the cellar for the winter months. They even let me have a small plot where I grew some popcorn, but then we couldn't afford butter to put on it after we popped it. Melvin and I thought we were lucky if we had a dime for a movie and a nickel for peanuts when we went to the movie on an occasional Friday night. And we didn't think to complain when our clothes were hand-me-downs. Once, when our gas was cut off because we couldn't pay the bills, my father, who was a kind of handyman, built a wood-fired stove on the basement floor. My mother did her cooking and baking there, and we called it our "Hoover oven." All the time I was going through school, I can remember only one Christmas when we had gifts. So those years of doing without convinced me later to become a Democrat.

During my father's retirement years, he worked as a boiler operator at Ashtabula General Hospital [now Ashtabula County Medical Center]. He would keep the door open there in the basement, and a family of raccoons made a habit of coming in while Dad was eating his evening lunch. They'd climb up on his lap and he'd give them a few bread crusts, and then they would go quietly out again. Somehow word got around, and a local newspaper reporter came in and took my father's picture while the raccoons were making one of their evening visits. I don't know what happened to that picture, but I wish I still had it.

I met my future wife when I was going to Harbor High School. I spotted her on the staircase and asked one of my friends if he knew her. He told me her name was Virginia Larson, and he suggested that I ask her to dance the next time we had one at school. Virginia had a Swedish father and a Finnish mother, and she was in the ninth grade at that time. But we didn't get serious until later, because I graduated in 1939—the eleventh in a class of ninety—and then I went off to Suomi College [now Finlandia University] in Hancock, Michigan. I had gotten a small scholarship, and I worked part time for my meals, and my brother, Matt, paid the rest of my expenses that totaled five hundred dollars. That was a paltry sum compared to today's standards. Then when I applied at Ohio State the next year, they told me my credits wouldn't transfer from Suomi, so my first year was a total loss, including the cost. Anyway, I started again as a freshman, and transferred my major to chemical engineering.

When I went for my college entrance physical examination, the doctors were amazed to find my right-sided heart. So they sent me to the hospital for full-length x-rays. After I waited about a week, they told me to report at the health office to review my films. Those doctors and nurses were standing around waiting to see what kind of strange guy was going to walk in, and it got me kind of worried about what they were going to tell me. But what they said was that not only my heart, but all of my internal organs were reversed, including the lobes of my brain. This condition is known as "situs inversus viscerum," and I wear this bracelet that tells that, in case I'm ever in an emergency situation. Yet I've always had good health, and I even excelled in track meets during my high-school years.

During World War II, three of my brothers served in the armed forces. Mauri was the only one who was in actual hand-to-hand combat, but after the war he was never able to talk about it. I tried to enlist several times during my college years, but when the recruiters heard I was studying chemical engineering, they wouldn't accept me. They just advised me to complete my education first. Finally, in 1944, I got my bachelor's degree in chemical engineering. After four years there of work and study, I was so relieved to be finished that I didn't stay around for the graduation. I had them mail me my diploma. I still think that a smaller college is better than a larger one, from every aspect.

I married Virginia Larson in 1945, and over the next ten years we had three children. Mike was born in 1948; Jonathan, in 1952; and Melinda, in 1955. Mike is now a purchasing manager for a sugar mill in Rodeo, California. Jonathan had a successful career with an engineering contractor, and he was just getting ready to retire when he passed away in 2002. Melinda is an associate professor in the Department of Natural Resources at Colorado State University in Fort Collins.

The most intriguing years during my engineering career were from 1975 to 1978, when I worked for the Fluor Corporation. They built the Iranian and Kuwaiti oil refineries and Pakistan's natural gas plants. I was based in their Tehran, Iran, office, and I traveled all over the Middle Eastern region. I saw vast differences between Middle Eastern cultures and those of the Western nations. It was disturbing to see the subservient position of women. Their husbands, by tradition, were chosen for them. For instance, I was once invited into the home of a Pakistani businessman who told me the story of his marriage: He was the manager of a tea plantation in India and was returning home for his vacation. His father met him at the airport with a distant relative who he introduced as the father of his future wife. The next day he met the man's daughter, and the day after that they were married. But he said his marriage was a happy one. Then another time I was invited out to dinner by an engineering executive. When I went to his home, his wife came into the room. She had on a gorgeous gown, and she was one of the most beautiful women I've ever seen, but she stood head and shoulders above her husband so I knew it must have been another arranged marriage.

In our country, dogs are considered man's best friend, but in Iran they run wild in the streets because they're thought to be unclean. When there get to be too many of them, the military is sent in to shoot the dogs and bury them. Their whole culture is alien to ours.

Virginia went with me, and we lived in a run-down villa surrounded by a high fence and a locked gate. The top of the block fence had sharp spikes and they were strung with barbed wire. We even had a German police dog to monitor the yard. They gave me a car to use, but with an Iranian driver. If a foreigner is involved in a car accident, no matter how it happens, the foreigner is automatically at fault. I made friends with some Iranians, though, when they finally learned to trust me. They said they liked Americans as individuals, but they disagreed with our government's policies when they affected their daily lives.

It was quite an experience shopping there, too. They use an abacus more than a cash register. I once saw a side of beef hanging outside a butcher shop. Inside, the meat looked as if it had been torn from a carcass and piled behind a glass counter. I asked for a steak, but I didn't really believe it was steak until it was cooked. Then we found it was pretty good, at that. There was a missionary and his wife in the same town who held nondenominational services for our military people stationed there. Virginia used to volunteer her help there.

We came back to the States twice during those years, just for meetings and seminars. Melinda was still a student then, but she was able to visit us twice. She made quite a stir because she's tall and has blonde hair; she really stood out among the Iranians.

We were glad to return home in 1979. I had worked in engineering for Ferguson/Morrison-Knudsen out of both their Cleveland and San Francisco offices. When I returned from Tehran, I still worked for Ferguson, but in business development instead of chemical engineering. I retired from their Cleveland office in 1986.

Virginia and I had been married for fifty-two years when she passed away in 1997. I began visiting with a longtime friend of Virginia's, Mildred Honkala. She had been widowed years before when her four sons were young, so she understood the grief I was going through. So that's how it started, and we got married about a year and a half later.

John and Mildred make their home in Painesville, Ohio. At the age of eighty-four (2005), John keeps active with golfing, and keeps informed by reading current and historical events. He enjoys traveling and gardening, and he maintains communication via his computer with his two children, grandchildren, and extended family. Most recently, John did an excellent job as master of ceremonies for the dedication and open house of the Finnish American Cultural Center on July 1, 2006.

Laina Eleanora Pouttu Sippola

Eleanor's father, Jaakko (Jacob) Pouttu, was born in Untamala, Finland, on March 14, 1872. Eleanor's mother, Adolfiina (Fiina) Rajamaki, was born in Ylihärmä, Finland, on October 6, 1871. Jacob and Fiina were married in 1896, and their first three children were born in Finland: Hilma Justiina, in 1897; Jaakob Jalmari (Elmer), in 1898; and Johan (John) Antoni, in 1899.

Jacob emigrated from Finland in March 1899. His passport was issued for five years, and his ticket price of 229 Finnish marks brought him from Hanko, Finland, to Ashtabula, Ohio. To save money, he traveled on a cattle boat. He later told how animal wastes would combine with human vomit in the hold of the ship whenever it rolled in rough seas. Jacob soon settled in Monessen, Pennsylvania (south of Pittsburgh), where he worked in a tin mill.

The following year, on June 12, 1900, Fiina and their three children sailed from Finland to the United States. Accompanying Fiina was her sixty-one-year-old mother, Maria Rajamaki, who came along to assist with the children.

They sailed on a ship of the White Star Line, and the price of Fiina's ticket with two of the children was twenty-four dollars. Her mother apparently carried one of the children with the name included on her passport and ticket. They arrived in Allenport, Pennsylvania, by train, the station nearest to Monessen.

The Pouttus had seven more children, all born in Monessen: Ksenja (Senia) Maria, born in 1901; Lempi (Mercie) Fretriika, in 1904; Eino Ilmari, 1906; Lilja (Lilly) Aina Emelia, 1907; Laina Eleanora (Eleanor) born February 12, 1910; Yrjo William, 1913; and William George, 1915. (The last two boys died in infancy.)

Maria traveled back and forth to Finland over the years to visit family left behind. She earned her own passage by knitting mittens and stockings, then selling them on the streets of Monessen. Eleanor remembered her grandmother walking down the street and knitting at the same time. Maria Rajamaki died in 1919, when she was eighty, and is buried in Monessen.

Although Eleanor's mother never learned English, her father spoke "Finglish," at work. Even with the vast differences between Finnish and English, men were forced to learn some English to understand instructions in their work environment. Years later, when Eleanor shopped for her parents, a grocery list her father wrote was saved. As the Finnish language has no "sh" or "ch" sound, nor "th," one item on the list was spelled "port sops tinlais" [thinly sliced pork chops]. Thus, he wrote Finglish as well as spoke it.

In 1920 the family moved to Ohio in search of farmland. The two older daughters, Hilma and Senia, were married by then, but would later move to Ohio. Eleanor was ten, and she remembered how flat Ohio seemed compared to the Pennsylvania hill towns. After a short while in Ashtabula Harbor, the family lived on several rented farms in Ashtabula County.

While living on Lindsley Farm in West Andover, Eleanor and her siblings walked one mile to a one-room schoolhouse, no matter what the weather, and without overshoes. The children milked cows, too, before and after school. Eleanor, Lilly, and Mercie shared a bed in the unheated second floor. When Mercie married and left home, the other two were delighted to have the additional space in bed.

The Pouttus were finally able to buy a small dairy farm on Route 7 in Williamsfield Township. The first house there was destroyed by fire, and the family cooked in the sauna and slept in the haymow of the barn until a new house was built. Eleanor attended Andover High School for two years, then dropped out and went to work weaving baskets at the Andover Basket

Factory. She was paid according to how many baskets she wove in one day, earning an average of two dollars a day, or about eight dollars per week.

Eleanor dated Isaac (Ike) Sippola, from Conneaut, for almost five years. They went to silent movies, dances, and visited her married sisters and members of his family. They were married in Ripley, New York, January 2, 1932. Eleanor went home to her parents for two weeks before she told them she had married.

These were Depression years, so Ike and Eleanor's first home was a two-room structure set in the woods of Ike's oldest sister's farm in Conneaut. Here their first child, Wesley Jerald (Jerry), was born on October 22, 1932. When the Sippola's second child, Noreen Adele, was born in an apartment on East 130th Street in Cleveland, Ike's sister, Virginia Johnson, called the doctor away from a New Year's Eve party to deliver the baby (January 1, 1935). Although Ike was a welder at that time, and then went to work as a house painter for his brother-in-law, Einar Johnson, a painting contractor, they found it increasingly difficult to pay rent in the city. Eleanor and the two children then moved in with her sister, Lilly, and her husband, Michael Kangas, on a rented farm not too far from the Pouttu farm. When Mike found work in another area, Eleanor and the children moved in with her parents. Ike continued working in Cleveland, boarding with one of his sisters, and coming home on weekends. Saturday evenings were lively at the Pouttu farm when Eleanor's siblings, those within driving distance, came to visit, drink coffee, and eat *nisua* that their mother baked every Saturday in her wood-fired stove. Ike brought along his accordion, playing polkas, waltzes, and marches for the others to enjoy. On Sunday mornings, the family listened to Reverend A. A. Harju's Finnish sermons on the radio and Ike read the "funnies" to his children. On Sunday nights, or early Monday morning, Ike returned to Cleveland once again.

When Eleanor was a child, Christmas was hardly observed, and she didn't receive a doll until her oldest sister, Hilma, was working and bought her one. Ike's family put up a tree, and their gifts consisted of mittens or stockings knitted by their mother and an orange. Even though money was scarce in the 1930s, Ike and Eleanor's children always received a few gifts from Santa. It was amusing to the adults when Jerry, as a toddler, spoke English to his parents, Finnish to his grandmother, and "Finglish" to his grandpa.

Because Ike and Eleanor had both been baptized and confirmed in the Lutheran church, they attended church services in area Finnish homes. The Lutheran minister came from Bethany Lutheran Church in Ashtabula on one

Sunday afternoon each month to lead these services, conduct confirmation classes, or baptize babies.

In January of 1938, the Sippolas purchased a seventy-five-acre farm on Ridge Road (Old Salt Road), Williamsfield Township. There was an old barn, and a house not lived in for years, that later would become the chicken coop. On weekends, Ike proceeded to tear down the old barn, using salvageable beams and wood to construct a new barn. A Cape Cod house was then built, set back from the unpaved road. Building continued without a mortgage. Materials were added when they could be paid for, and volunteer help was obtained from brothers and brothers-in-law, whenever they were available.

The Sippola's third child, Linda Lou, was born in her grandparents' home on October 21, 1940, and the family moved into the new house on November 16, 1940. Ike continued working in Cleveland, coming home on weekends. Eleanor was there alone with the three children, with no central heating, indoor plumbing, or electricity. On the weekends, when Ike returned, she could use the car for grocery shopping. Gradually, over the years, the house was completed, but a bathroom wasn't installed until 1946, and a telephone wasn't installed until 1950. Ike was too old to serve in World War II, but he worked in a war plant while farming during those years.

The Sippolas acquired milking cows and began shipping daily two or three ten-gallon cans. Ike sold his accordion to buy one cow. They also raised chickens and often had enough eggs to sell at the grocery store. Ike began working for a painting contractor in Warren in 1941 and was then able to be home each evening. He and Eleanor hand-milked the cows, morning and night. Eleanor churned butter for their own use.

The children attended Williamsfield School from grades one through twelve and were transported by bus. School was in session from 8:45 A.M. to 3:30 P.M. for all grades. Two grades were housed in one room until high school, when each grade had a separate homeroom.

In late fall of 1944, Ike fell ill with rheumatic fever. Antibiotics weren't yet available to the general public, and he received only sulfa drugs. Eleanor and Jerry (then twelve) took care of the feeding and milking of cows and other chores. That spring, they fitted the fields and planted the crops with some help from Eleanor's brothers, Eino and Elmer. Jerry missed forty days of school in junior high, yet managed to earn all As. It was summer before Ike was able to resume some of the lighter chores and even longer before he could work again outside the farm.

Eleanor worked cleaning cabins many years at the Pymatuning State Parks. This was seasonal work, mainly on summer Saturdays, except when the cleaning ladies tackled spring cleaning. We can be sure that Eleanor; her sister, Mercie Kangas-Sevon; and sister-in-law, Jennie Pouttu, gave the cabins a thorough Finnish cleaning.

Eleanor became a young grandmother when her first grandson, Alan Sippola, was born in 1951, when she was forty-one. Noreen's four sons, and Linda's one daughter and two sons added an additional seven grandchildren. On many occasions, over the years, the grandchildren enjoyed their visits at the farm when their parents were working or on vacation. Thanksgiving Days were always spent at the Sippola farm. The women each brought food to contribute and then took turns hand-washing dishes after the meal. The men and boys (when they got older) often went deer hunting there in the woods.

After Ike retired, the couple drove to Florida to stay for a few weeks during winters. Ike tuned accordions and refinished antique furniture for local people, and Eleanor continued with seasonal work at the park.

Because of damage to his heart from two episodes of rheumatic fever, Ike died of a myocardial infarction on September 7, 1976, a month before his seventy-second birthday. Eleanor remained on the farm with her son and daughter-in-law living next door. She flew to Finland in 1977 with her daughter and son-in-law, Linda and John Riddell, and their two sons. She continued working at the park until age seventy, when she was diagnosed with lung and bone cancer; this came as a shock because she had always had good health and habits. She chose not to have chemotherapy or radiation but tried some nontraditional methods. Nevertheless, she gradually weakened. She died on November 1, 1982, at the age of seventy-two, leaving her three children, eight grandchildren, and three great-grandchildren. The Sippolas are buried in Williamsfield's Center Cemetery, with an accordion engraved on their headstone.

Linda Riddell obtained passport records from the National Archives, Helsinki, Finland, on one of her visits that provided background information for the Pouttu family. She and Noreen and Jerry contributed these accounts of their mother's life.

Ashtabula River near the lakefront in 1875, when Finnish immigrants began arriving in Ashtabula Harbor. Now only pleasure boats cruise the river. (Photo courtesy of Petros Collection)

Early Finnish crew of ore shovelers with Paul Eskelin, gang boss, center front. (Photo courtesy of Harland Myllamaki and FACC)

Pontoon bridge spanning the Ashtabula River, ca. 1885. Boats are both sail and steam, and coal cars are seen in the foreground. (Photo courtesy of Petros Collection)

Russell Holmstrom's maternal grandparents, Antti and Maria (Karhu) Hill, on their wedding day in 1894 in Conneaut, Ohio. (Photo courtesy of Russell Holmstrom and FACC)

Kaisa (Malkamaki) and Isaak Sippola with first two children, John and Elizabeth, in 1899 in Conneaut, Ohio (eleven more children followed). Kaisa was twenty-six years old in this photo but appeared much older in her somber dress and severe hairdo. (Family photo)

Antti and Maria (Toppari) Laituri in their 1901 wedding portrait, taken in Conneaut, Ohio. (Photo courtesy of John Laituri)

Sovinto (Harmony) Hall was constructed in 1901 as a temperance hall and then became a cultural and recreational center. Its use diminished after World War II, and it was demolished in the early 1960s. The first Bethany Lutheran Church appears in the next block of Joseph Avenue, Ashtabula Harbor. (Photo courtesy of Petros Collection)

Facing page: Undated photo (looking northeast toward the swing bridge) of early Bridge Street, Ashtabula Harbor, in the horse and buggy days, with trolley tracks in the center. (Photo courtesy of Petros Collection)

Victor and Wilhamiina (Sippola) Kaura and young Oliver, ca. 1913. Both parents played musical instruments, and Oliver became a musician, band conductor, choral director, and instructor. (Photo courtesy of Elizabeth Karbacka)

Early-Twentieth-Century Arrivals, 1900–1909

The greatest influx of Finnish immigrants to northeast Ohio arrived just after the turn of the twentieth century. These years ushered in a building boom of temperance halls, churches, homes, and saunas.

To combat the evils of drunkenness and wages lost in the saloons, a temperance movement began in 1885. Men were encouraged to sign sobriety pledges and to attend meetings. As membership grew, temperance halls were constructed to house lending libraries, invite musical involvement and athletic competitions, and provide other means of socializing within the Finnish community. In Ashtabula Harbor, Sovinto Hall was dedicated on New Year's Eve 1902. The hall measured 110 feet by 50 feet wide, with a height of 40 feet, all at a cost of fourteen thousand dollars. A tower was added that contained a four-faced clock, made in Finland, and required winding only three times a year. This illuminated clock could be seen at night by Great Lakes' sailors. For nearly fifty years Sovinto was a thriving community and cultural center, but the World War II years and the decade following brought about the hall's demise. Social needs were soon fulfilled by high schools' drama, music, and sports departments, along with commercial entertainment, and the grand old structure was demolished in 1961.

Membership continued to thrive in the Lutheran churches once they were established and constructed. In 1881 a visiting minister arrived in Ashtabula, followed by several short-term ministers. Then the first permanent Lutheran minister, Abel Kivioja, arrived from Finland in 1891. By July 1893 the first Bethany Lutheran Church had been built and was dedicated with all services conducted in Finnish—the primary language used by the first and second generations in their homes.

Although there were no official signs, the Finns remained clustered in their own communities, such as "Finn Town" in Ashtabula Harbor and "Finn Hollow" in Fairport Harbor. Some Finnish men brought their carpentry skills from Finland or acquired them here. Soon they were building homes, retail specialty shops, businesses, and additional temperance and socialist meeting halls.

Public saunas were also built to accommodate those who didn't have space for one in their backyard. These saunas were often viewed with a certain curiosity, if not disfavor, by the earlier Western Reserve settlers and other ethnic groups. They believed them to be places of torment and self-flagellation instead of the centuries-old innocuous custom that was considered a necessity to the Finnish people.

Matt Luoma

My mother was born in Ashtabula Harbor. Her name was Filda Heikkila, but she went by Matilda. My father, with my same name—Matt Luoma—came from Kaustinen in Finland. He said they stayed a week at Ellis Island to straighten up everything and find out who was backing them in the States. He must have come here in the early 1900s. He came to Ashtabula because other people from that section of Finland came here before. My father and mother met in Ashtabula, and they got married here, but I don't know what date.

I'm the oldest, and I was born on October 15, 1908, when the folks were living on Oak Street. Then there was my brother, Ernest, and my sister, Eleanor. My father worked on the docks for a long time, and then he worked at the New York Central Railroad; he was a car repairman. Mother worked doing housework for the city manager and for one of the doctors, and other people.

I went to school in the Washington and Jackson buildings and then graduated from Harbor High School in 1927. Our church was Bethany Lutheran. The Finnish people used to have picnics at the "squirrel woods," where Bethany is now. My father played trumpet and violin with the Humina Band. The Humina Band was a great thing. I used to go up there every Friday night when my father rehearsed, and they were good. I often wondered where all those old-timers learned to play like that. They didn't have to take a backseat to anybody. Even us school kids would have to go and practice with the Humina Band. When we sang with them we had so many rests and notes, and a couple of the Finn guys would call out the rests, real loud, saying the numbers in Finnish. We used to sing "Down in the Valley," and "I Want a Girl Just Like the Girl That Married Dear Old Dad." We'd sing that kind of song.

Growing up, we played baseball, basketball, and we were all golfers, but when my mother and father said to do something, we had to do it. Ernie and I used to like to play basketball Saturday mornings at Harbor High School. Many mornings we'd go there and forget we had chores to do, so that night we didn't get to go to the Palace Theatre, either. Every Saturday we were supposed to do a certain job.

We had some of the best boxers and wrestlers come to compete at Sovinto Hall. Some of our Finn guys used to wrestle with the big shots. My brother was a good baseball player. My brother and Howard Joki and Kelly Altonen would make good outfielders in Cleveland right now.

We went to Haywood Beach every summer. That was like a resort for people, and every weekend people would gather there. My brother and I went, and my folks also, but we were with our gang, and they were with their gang. Modern Woodmen picnic grounds was a big place where old Camp Luther used to be—out on Lake Road East, along the lake. Later, we'd start swimming at Walnut Beach and we'd have trunks because everybody else did. We'd always have to wear a T-shirt, too. Coleman had coal yards, and in winter we'd ride with his sleigh. A couple guys had sleighs that would peddle their groceries and we'd ride with them. We went to dances at the halls, and to Geneva-on-the-Lake where the bigger-named bands came. They had three dance halls there. We used to go to the Torps hall when there was the Socialist movement, and we'd play basketball. One guy warned us about their kind, because he knew all of us kids went to church and Sunday school, and he told us, "Don't listen to their stuff; they're Communists." We heard a lot of stuff, and learned what was really happening with them people.

I used to like to make that trip to Lampela's store with my father on payday. When Lampela would get paid, he'd usually give the kids candy or an apple or something like that.

My first job was a caddy at the Ashtabula Country Club. Then I worked at the greenhouse. After high school graduation, I worked at the Hide and Leather uptown, and was lucky to get a job. A lot of Finns and Italians worked there. I think four Jews even worked in there. I once played on the same golf course as Jackie Gleason in Florida. He said we must be all ex-caddies, the way we played. Even the pros at the Country Club told us we could come play there anytime because we behaved better than their members did.

I worked with the CCC [Civilian Conservation Corps], and that was one of the best things we ever had. They should have that for the kids today. We worked in the forest cutting trees down; we built roads; and we even had our own stone quarry. People would think we had an easy life, but we had a worse inspection than they had in the army. We had a navy commander for our commanding officer, and we had an army lieutenant that was in charge of our food and stuff. Our forest rangers knew right away who were the city boys who never swung a hatchet or a shovel. Our commander would ask how many guys would take a steady KP job or be cooks, and we knew right away it would be the city guys. We were lucky that some guys were good cooks. Sandfield was our first-aid man, and many days we didn't want to go work in the woods, so we'd tell him we want to be on sick call; he had four bunks in there so we had a place to sleep. We were always the first guys in the kitchen, and the cooks would fix us good food because we were sick.

Every morning our captain would come up, and we would have swept our barracks, and we would have to have everything cleaned up—the floor swept, and our shoes had to be polished, and then our clothes had to be hung a certain way. So everything was in order. It was just like the army, and all young kids today should have that. Our gang went once to California to work. My mother got thirty dollars a month, and I only got five. That kept my mother going, and she could make better use of it than me because we had our clothes, our eats, and a place to sleep. We built the park in Peninsula [Ohio], too, and we worked some on building Pymatuning Lake.

I was in the army during World War II. I was stationed in Panama, where we loaded ships with big cannons, airplanes, trucks, and everything for the invasion of Sicily. Some people thought the guys in the army had it easy. Well, we didn't have to march like the infantry did, but we worked night and day just loading the ships up. Then, when the war was over in Europe, we went to Panama and loaded supplies on all those ships that were going to the Pacific. I liked Panama, and we had a good gang there.

I made sure my mother got a letter from me every month. One day I got a letter from Mr. Wenner, and our captain came to see me. He said that I must have gotten an important letter, so I let him read it when I got through, and he said, "That man must have been very well educated." And I said, "He is superintendent of our school." When I went home on furlough, about four or five of us guys went to see Wenner, and he thought that was great. He told us they were going to have a recognition evening at the church across from the high school, and he wanted us boys to be there. So we went and had dinner there, and Wenner was bragging that some of the boys had come to see him, and he told them to treat us well. We had a nice time there.

One New Year's Eve, some of us guys had gone to the Iroquois Club and had a few beers. Then somebody got the bright idea of going to the six o'clock early service at Bethany. Otto Maki was the pastor then, and he said that last night we were drinking, and now we are in church. When he made a statement like that, he thought we were doing a good thing. We had always gone before, and we thought we were just as good as the rest of the people because we hadn't done anything bad.

After the war I worked on the Pennsylvania ore docks. Matt Kujala [contractor] got a gang of about ten or twelve of us to help build the new Bethany church [1954–55] every Saturday morning. You should have seen when we put the roof on with big planks, and then we would be pushing all the shingles up there. We put a steel drain pipe in the basement, and Kujala said we got everything level and had done a good job. The women even made lunch for us in the basement of the old Bethany church.

Charlie Potti [undertaker] had an old office—it's a bank now—and we used to play cards there. One night Jack Quirk drank a little too much and Charlie thought he'd play a trick on him. We carried Jack and put him in a coffin, and in the morning he wondered where in the hell he was. He sobered up after that and quit drinking. Then Jack and his wife went to Painesville and had a coffee shop, and he stayed sober.

Some of us retired guys used to meet for coffee at Lakeway Restaurant, and we called ourselves the "Finn Mafia." Ray Koski made a sketch of us "charter members" one time, and I think that sketch is still hanging in the restaurant.

Matt married Helen Thurman on September 9, 1966, when he was fifty-eight. They had no children. Matt worked for the True Temper Corporation until he retired. His mother died in 1972, and Helen died in 1988. Matt spent his last days at the Austinburg Rehabilitation Center. He died there on June 23, 2001, at the age of ninety-two.

Martha Lilya

My father, Johan Lilya, came to the United States from Kiuruvesi, Finland, in the early 1900s. My mother, Ruusa Pranny, came from Laihia. She had finished her schooling in Finland and was eighteen when she came here. She said she was sick the entire time she was on the boat coming to America. She came to Ashtabula because her uncle, who was already there, sent her the fifteen dollars for her passage. My mother got her citizenship papers when she was a little older.

My mother and father met in Ashtabula and were married there in 1904. They first lived on what used to be called lower Oak Street [West Eighth Street]. They always rented a place, and never owned a home. My father was a tailor before he came to this country, so he worked in a tailor's shop on Bridge Street with four or five other men.

I was the oldest of three. I was born in Ashtabula Harbor on February 14, 1906. My sister, Helen (Price), was born in September of 1907. Then Wayne, my brother, was born in 1910, and our father died when Wayne was just nine months old. My mother was only twenty-seven when she became a widow, so she had quite a load on her hands, but she made it. I have a photo of my father's funeral carriage that was pulled by white horses. It was taken in front of the old Bethany Lutheran Church. And what I most treasure is the christening gown that all three of us children wore when we were baptized.

My mother's mother, Maria, came to live with us after my father died. But she was here only a short time and got sick, and then she died in 1912. I remember when my grandmother used to comb my hair and then braid it. She really hurt my scalp, because she put the braids so tight, you know. I must have had a sensitive head. My mother didn't go to work right away, so she must have had enough to sustain us for a while. After that, she had babysitters for us.

My mother used to go to different things at Sovinto Hall, like plays and concerts. And we used to listen to the Humina Band when they practiced behind Sovinto Hall. We went to the Harbor schools and to Bethany Lutheran Church. My mother used to take us to the Modern Woodmen picnic grounds and to the church picnics in old Bethany's yard. We used to go to the movie theaters on Bridge Street, and I think the admission was five cents during the week and ten cents when we went on the weekends. We visited ice-cream parlors, too, and in winter we used to sled-ride a lot. Everybody seemed to have a sled, and we'd find a hill somewhere. I remember our mother taking us to Woodland Beach Park on Sundays, which was quite a thrill. We always celebrated holidays by visiting friends.

I remember the stores we went to. Mr. Salgen was a Finn who had a store called the "Racket Store." He had a little bit of everything, like hardware and kitchen dishes. Hamalainen had a grocery store, and he had some foods stored in barrels. It was located just about where Chapman's store is now. Then there was Lundi's Meat Market, and I remember the Sippola Bakery. Jacob

Sippola was a big, tall man, and there was that Alice Sippola; I remember her. Everybody who went into that building got good stuff.

My first job was babysitting and doing light housework during the summers. After I graduated from Harbor High School in 1924, I worked at the Electric Laundry as a bookkeeper. I answered the phone, too, and waited on people. I worked there for many years. During the Depression, my mother worked at the Electric Laundry, too, and she kept working there for years. Of course, neither one of us worked full time during the Depression. I remember there was a time when you couldn't buy sugar, but my mother was able to buy hard candy, which she used in place of a sugar cube in her coffee.

I moved into a house on West Eighth Street in 1959. I lived in the upstairs apartment and rented the first floor out. Wayne worked in a war plant during World War II. He never married, so he came to live with me later on, until he died in 1989 when he was seventy-nine.

After the Electric Laundry burned down, I went to work as a clerk for the city auditor. I retired from there in 1970. I was a member of the Finlandia Foundation, and I was a member of Bethany all my life.

Martha lived alone until she was taken to the Ashtabula County Medical Center. She died there on February 2, 2003, at the age of ninety-seven. She was survived by two nephews, Robert and Richard Price.

Arvo Johannas Ritari

My father was Johan Rikart (Richard) Ritari, and he came here from Laihia, Finland, around 1900. He came to Conneaut because he heard there was work there at the docks. My mother's name was Lempi Sundberg, and she came to Conneaut, too, from Ortisvala. My mother worked as a maid for a long time in one place. I don't know how my folks met, but they were married in Conneaut.

By the time I was born, on July 27, 1905, we were living on Broad Street. I had four brothers, and Eino is the only one living. Then there was Lauri, Ilmari, and Rhiner. My sisters are Lillian and Helen—both living. We all went to the Dean Avenue School, and then to Conneaut High School. It was a good mile from our house to the high school.

We belonged to the old Finnish Lutheran Church on Broad Street. I went to

Sunday School and the first day they wanted to know how I could read Finn. At that time I don't think I knew a word of English, but I could read Finn as fast as I could talk. We had Sunday summer school in them days; used to be the minister's wife was the teacher. I went to confirmation school there, too, and was confirmed when I was about fifteen.

I started going fishing with my father when I was seven. We'd get up at four in the morning and get back at noon. We caught pike and perch and gave most of them away. I made two cents a quart for picking berries. I made about a dollar a day because I picked so many quarts. Then, after six o'clock, I'd go down to the park and order an ice-cream cone. I really enjoyed that. I used to buy all my winter clothes with that money, too.

We didn't celebrate any holidays because we were a poor family. They came here with empty pockets, and that's the way they left. But my mother made Finnish foods like rice pudding, stew, and she baked all our bread and *nisua*. I don't think I ate store-bought bread until I was maybe eighteen or nineteen years old. I used to have some family pictures, but we had a fire back in—I don't know when—but that's how my pictures were lost.

We made our own fun when we were growing up. Oh, boy—swimming, horse-shoe pitching, hide-and-seek. I had an old rowboat once, but I never had my own fishing pole. I always fished with my hat.

When I was sixteen, in 1921, I was an apprentice for railroad car repairing. I lost my job during the Depression, but they called me back again because I was such a good inspector and they needed one. The superintendent of the car department knew that I knew my business because I had worked with him on a lot of special jobs. We were lucky to have jobs during World War II. We were classified special so nobody else could fill them. I was an inspector in the car shop where they repaired freight trains. The Nickel Plate [Railroad] had a good shop there, now it's just a pass-through station with no repair work at all. They had sixty-eight men repairing there before.

They used to have train wrecks, too. One time there was pigs in the cars, and they were hurt so bad they had to shoot them all. Those pigs started to rot right away, and it stunk so bad, boy, you couldn't stay there. I went back after a few hours and they were all gone, and they said some slaughterhouse took them because they weren't fit to eat—the blood was all let out. They had cows—steers—too, from that wreck, and I don't know how many yards were filled with those steers, and that was right in town.

My first wife was Olga Lampinen, and we had one son, Allen. We lived on Amboy Road, where we had a garden of potatoes, tomatoes, and corn.

We had a cow when we first moved out there. It was a Jersey, and we had all the milk we could use, so we gave all the milk she wanted to a widow lady across the street.

I didn't build my first house. Way back before 1900, up until about 1910, they had this long pier built way back there that started to collect sand. It collected sand for about a half a mile, and they built houses in there. So my first house was moved there. It was a beach house, stacked up the hill on Dean Avenue. Then lightning struck it and it burned down. I built my second house in the summer of 1935, and I built the sauna in 1944.

I went to Finland thirteen times. The first time I rented a car, but it doesn't pay. There was a limit you could drive, and I think I drove three hundred miles over the limit. I had to pay almost as much for those three hundred miles as for all the others. So then I started buying a car and selling it before I came home.

After Olga died, I met and married Siiri Kotamaki during one of my Finland trips. Both my wives are gone now.

Arvo retired in 1967 after forty-three years with the Nickel Plate Railroad. He was a member of Conneaut's Good Shepherd Lutheran Church, and was the oldest member of the Kaleva Lodge in Fairport Harbor. Arvo died in the Ashtabula County Nursing Home on December 10, 1997, at the age of ninety-one. Survivors included his son, three grandchildren, six great-grandchildren, and his two sisters.

Ellen Susan Kesatie Sippola

My mother, Mari (Maria) Kateriina Riisio, was born in Kauhava, Finland, on March 30, 1881. Around 1900, when she was nineteen, she traveled to America on a cattle boat. To earn her way over here she helped care for the animals. She came with a pack, probably a birch-bark one, where she packed dried bread and dried fish for her meals. My daughter still has this pack.

My father, Salomon Emanuel Kesatie, was born December 19, 1880, in Ylihärmä. He left there around 1900, too, and went to Conneaut first, where our aunt Betti was, then he went to Monessen, Pennsylvania. In Monessen, he met and married Iihanelma Hatunen. She was from Karsamäki. They had one daughter, Impi Elizabeth, born in 1903, but Iihanelma died in September 1904. She was buried in Monessen. Then my father's half-sister, Betti Kujala, became Impi's foster mother. It was our aunt Betti who sent Dad the ticket to come here; at that time, Russia's czar was drafting Finnish men to fight in the Russo-Japanese War, but he left so he didn't have to go in the Russian army.

My father then married my mother—his second wife. They had three children who were born in Monessen: Lempi Maria was born in 1906; then John, but he died in infancy; and Toivo Emanuel, born in 1909.

My father's last name when he came to this country was Aulin, and when he worked in the tin-plate mine in Monessen the shift foreman would call: "Aulin, Aulin!" My dad thought that sounded too much like "all in," so he changed his name to Kesatie, which was actually his stepfather's last name. Anyway, he worked nine years in that tin mill and began to have health problems. So a doctor told him that if he didn't get out of the mill the dust in there would kill him. So in 1911 our family moved to Lake Road, east of Conneaut, then shortly after that, a 160-acre farm went up for sale on Childs Road on the Ohio-Pennsylvania line. And that's where we'd live for twenty-eight years.

The rest of us nine kids were born on that farm: Andrew Emil, born in 1911; Salomon Evert, in 1913; Martha Kathryn, 1915; then me—Ellen Susan, December 6, 1916; Jacob Edwin, 1918; Sylvia Viola, 1920; Viljo Einar, 1921; Elsa Wilhelmina, 1924; and Martin Erland, 1926.

Of course, at first, they had no electricity, no indoor plumbing, and no furnace. There was the house, a barn, tool shed, and a couple other smaller buildings—like a chicken coop—but they said everything needed paint. One thing Dad built, though, was a sauna building. My dad had to start from scratch: he had to buy cows, horses, wagons, and all that farm machinery.

My mother did just about everything. She milked the cows and took care of all us kids. She kept a big garden and could cut grass and weeds with a scythe. She sewed all our clothes on a treadle sewing machine, and she was always knitting something. She washed clothes in a copper tub set on a fire outside, and they had to carry all the water from a well. She did all the cooking and baking with a wood-fired kitchen stove, and she made rugs on a loom that my dad built. She used to go into town with a horse and buggy to sell or trade her homemade butter and eggs for other groceries. We didn't get our Ford pickup truck until 1929, and my oldest brother probably drove our mother into town with that.

We went to Carnegie School, which was a one-room schoolhouse on the corner of Rudd and Lake Roads. Then, in the fall of 1924, we were transferred to a school in West Springfield, Pennsylvania. A kid hack pulled by horses brought us there. By 1930 our driver bought a flatbed truck; he put benches in it for seats, but if the roads were too muddy or snowy, he used the horses again.

We went to the Finnish Lutheran Church in Conneaut. It was a long walk there, especially in winter, so Dad got us together on Sunday mornings at home and read to us from the Bible.

After we'd been on the farm about eight years, the barn got hit by lightning and a lot of machinery and equipment were lost in the fire. My dad had to buy some new equipment that next year. Instructions for putting the equipment together were printed in English, but he somehow managed to get it done.

In our south pasture there was a section along Turkey Creek where we went swimming. Us girls couldn't afford bathing suits, so Mother had us each wear an old dress with the hem pinned up between our legs. We used our imagination and thought of a lot of things that were fun to do. My brother was good at carpentry, so he made a frame with a roof on it and we covered it with burlap. In the wintertime our father would make a hill for us by piling snow on the shed roof, then gradually bringing the snow down to make a hill for us to slide on.

Christmas was a fun time. We'd go out and find our own tree from the woods and bring it home, then Father would put it in a stand. We were like the other old-timers, putting candles on it for light. My father would have a couple pails of water ready in case we had a fire. The candles were lit for just a short time on Christmas Eve. Then either my mother or father would dress like Santa Claus. They would give an excuse, like one of them had to go to the barn because a cow was sick, then a little later Santa would come in. Mother made us *nisua* boys, similar to gingerbread with raisin buttons and raisin eyes, and we each got one gift. One year I got a teddy bear, and I had never seen one in my life. When I saw that fur I got scared and got up and went running. I don't think I ever did touch it!

But we had chores to do, too. Our brothers had to cut the wood for the stoves, to make fence posts, and to heat the sauna. And all of us hoed the cornfield and our big vegetable garden, so that was a big job. We used to pick wild strawberries by the railroad track until we planted our own strawberry patch, and there were a lot of blackberries to be picked. They said I was the champion strawberry picker. The older we got, the more work we had to do.

After I graduated from Conneaut High School in 1934, I worked for a crippled woman who was in a wheelchair. I helped with cooking and cleaning. My oldest sister was working in Cleveland, so I went there, too, and got a job taking care of Mel Harder's three-year-old daughter. [At that time, Mel Harder was a well-known pitcher for the Cleveland Indians.] I'd take her out for walks and play with her in the sandbox. The lady there did the cooking, but I had to peel the potatoes and carrots, and help with whatever she was going to cook.

I married Allen Sylvester Sippola in 1938. We first lived upstairs of his folks' bakery on Buffalo Street in Conneaut. Allen was working as an oiler on the Great Lakes' freighters. He did this for eight years, but after our second son was born, he decided not to go back on the lake boats. We had six children: Gail Ellen (Moulton), born in 1939; Errol Allan, 1940; Jacob Sylvester, 1943; Roger Paul, 1944; Saima Maria (Kelley), 1945; and Glenn George, 1947.

Allen studied and got his stationary engineer's license that got him a job at a Grand River soybean plant. Then, from 1952 until 1963, we owned the Fairport steam bath on Eagle Street in Fairport Harbor. In 1963 and '64, we managed an eight-unit motel in Fort Lauderdale, Florida. Allen died in Florida in March of 1967 after his aorta ruptured. We brought him back up here to Ashtabula to be buried.

After Allen died, I worked in a factory for a while, and I did housecleaning for a while. I had a girlfriend who worked at Andrews School for Girls in Willoughby [Ohio], and she said, "That would be the perfect place for you, Ellen. When you're ready to go, I'll take you." So I agreed, and worked there for seventeen years, beginning in 1972. I was a house mother for about ten years, then I was the health-center mother for the last seven years.

I was always interested in watercolors, so when I was at Andrews I took painting lessons at Willoughby's Fine Arts Center. I won a ribbon at the Lake County Fair one year for my watercolor picture of an old barn.

After Ellen retired in 1989, she moved into an apartment in Breckenridge Village, Willoughby. She died at age eighty-six on November 4, 2002, and is buried next to her husband, Allen Sippola, in Greenlawn Memory Gardens, North Kingsville, Ohio.

Marilyn Ruuska Salo

I was born in Ashtabula on July 9, 1933, but all four of my grandparents emigrated from Finland. My paternal grandfather, Henry Ruuska, emigrated from Aluvas in the early 1900s. My paternal grandmother, Helja Kivenmäki, emigrated from Karstula, also during the early 1900s. She was just sixteen years old when she left, and she traveled with a friend who ended up becoming her sister-in-law. My grandmother's mother had other children, but she was devastated when her daughter left. When it came time to say goodbye, her mother just put her hand up and cried and couldn't say a thing. Then she went to bed for several days.

My grandmother and her friend went through Ellis Island, then took a train to Ashtabula Harbor because my grandmother had a sister who was already living there. But this sister had a husband and a family of her own, so she gave my grandmother some money and told her to go to Cleveland to find work there and didn't offer to have her stay with them.

So there they were—two teenagers in a strange land. They didn't speak a word of English, and they were going to a strange city where they didn't know anybody. Can you imagine? Anyway, they found work in boarding houses as maids, then they eventually came back to Ashtabula and found work.

My grandmother met and married my grandfather, Henry Ruuska, around 1905, and they had three children: Elmer, Martin (my father), and Mary. After they were married, my grandfather worked on the docks, and my grandmother was a housewife who cooked on a coal stove, both winter and summer.

My Ruuska grandparents never owned a home; they rented apartments instead. They once lived upstairs of the same apartment building where my aunt and uncle lived. They used to bang on the water pipes to send messages back and forth. They didn't have phones, and their apartment was right above my aunt's, so they'd bang on the water pipes to communicate. Each number of bangs had a different meaning. These four-unit apartments were what you might call "cold-water flats." They usually went to a public sauna, but often sponge-bathed in the kitchen sinks. And they went to the basement, where two partitioned-off toilets were shared by the four apartments.

I have many fond memories of my Ruuska grandmother. She was very fun-loving. She lived to be ninety and is buried in Ridgeview Cemetery in Ashtabula.

My maternal grandparents, William and Mary (Hassinen) Bihlajama, were married in Finland in 1893 with a "crown wedding." On her wedding day, my grandmother wore a crown that had been passed down for generations. It was an old custom and an important tradition. People who had crown weddings were usually well-to-do.

My Bihlajama grandparents had one child, Matthew, when they immigrated to America during the late 1890s. And my grandmother was pregnant with their second child when they left Finland. They stayed first in New York for a while, and my grandmother earned money by doing housework for wealthy families. She learned some English then, too, so by the time they came to Ashtabula Harbor she spoke English fairly well and was often called upon to act as an interpreter for Finnish doctors.

My Bihlajama grandparents had seven more children after coming to this country: John, Hilda, June, Urho, Arthur (who died in infancy), Signe (my mother), and Helmi.

My uncle Matthew's nickname was "Pickles." He was short and heavy. He quit school early so he could work and earn money for the family. His earnings helped buy luxury items such as a Victrola and a radio. In those days, most immigrant families didn't have nice things like that.

Grandpa Bihlajama was a carpenter by trade, and he built a house for his family. He also built furniture and a wooden rug loom for my grandmother. She spent many hours in the basement weaving rugs or knitting. Whenever I visited my grandmother, there always seemed to be a group of ladies downstairs talking and helping her wind rag strips into balls for her rug weaving. Her daughter later continued with the rug weaving.

Grandma Bihlajama made traditional Finnish foods, such as coffee bread, rice pudding, small sausages, and fish soup with potatoes. Sometimes I helped her in the kitchen. She gave me a bowl and some flour and water, and I mixed them together and made a mess. Then my grandfather would suggest that I toss it out the window to feed the birds. My grandmother Bihlajama also had a slew of home remedies to cure ailments. She used ginger for an upset stomach, rhubarb as a spring tonic and for constipation, and used camphorated oil for ear infections.

My cousins and I went to play in the city dump that was behind my grandparents' house. We hunted for tossed-out treasures, and sometimes we'd find jewelry. Or we swung from one side of the dump to the other on rope swings tied to a tree. We slid down the hill on pieces of tin. Those big cans that Spam used to come in made great tin slides after we flattened them out.

My Bihlajama grandparents owned a milk cow, and every day the kids had to lead it to pasture on the corner of Ohio Avenue and Carpenter Road. Many local families lead their cows there to graze.

At Christmastime, my parents, aunts, uncles, and cousins gathered at Grandma Bihlajama's table for simple Finnish meals of coffee, cake, sandwiches, soup and coffee bread. On New Year's Eve, Grandpa Bihlajama dropped pieces of hot lead into a bucket of cold water. We would all peer into the bucket to see what shapes the cooling lead formed, because the shapes were supposed to forecast the future for the new year.

I remember going to someone's house after a death to view the body before the funeral. In those days, a body was often laid out at home instead of going to a funeral parlor. Funeral services were in Finnish, and the church offered two Sunday services, one in English and one in Finnish. My Bihlajama grandparents always spoke Finnish, and they always attended the Finnish service, because they were active member of Bethany Lutheran Church. In those days, ministers were very firm and strict. There were big confirmation classes, and most kids were confirmed around age fourteen.

My grandma Bihlajama died in 1943 and is buried in Edgewood Cemetery. Grandpa Bihlajama married twice more after she died, but Grandma had been eight years older than Grandpa, so I guess he was still young enough to marry again. Grandpa Bihlajama died in 1955.

My father, Martin Ruuska, was born August 6, 1907, in Ashtabula Harbor. My mother, Signe Bihlajama, was born August 1, 1906, also in Ashtabula. My parents were longtime sweethearts because they both grew up on Cherry Street [West Ninth Street] and knew each other from the time they were children.

My dad often went to Woodland Beach Park [an amusement park], but his family never had anything to do with the Socialist movement. My dad told us that when he was about eight years old he and some friends hopped a ship as it was leaving the harbor but were discovered before the ship got very far out.

Another time he was standing in front of a bank with some other boys when the bank got robbed. Years later, one of the men told my dad he was afraid he was going to be hit by gunshot because he was standing so close to the bank. My dad quit school after the ninth grade so he could go to work. His first job was at a greenhouse, then he worked at Ashtabula's Orange Crush Bottling Plant. When he was thirty-five, he got a job at the Pennsylvania-Youngstown-Ashtabula [PY&A] ore docks.

My mom and dad were married on September 29, 1928. They eloped to Ripley, New York, which was a popular place to get married then. My uncle Urho and my aunt Mary drove them there because Urho had a car and, on the way, they were stopped for speeding. Then my parents got married in a Presbyterian church. They first lived in an apartment upstairs of the Bihlajama's that cost them seven dollars a month.

I was born in 1933 and was their only child. During World War II, my dad was drafted. He sold his car, expecting to leave, but at the last minute they lowered the age limit and he was too old to go—much to my mother's relief.

When I was a young girl, we spent a lot of time at Sovinto Hall. My parents were wonderful dancers; they could waltz, polka, and square-dance. They did it all, and I liked to watch them go around the floor. There were always big crowds of people there, and everyone was very lively and fun loving at the dances. The men and boys went to the hall, too, to shoot pool and play basketball. Kids gathered there to roller skate and buy candy that was sold in the basement. The men always smoked in the basement, and it smelled like smoke down there all the time. The basement was an athletic room; the first floor was for dances; and there was also a ballroom upstairs.

For a while, my aunt Hilda—my mother's sister—and her husband, Elden Cain, lived on the top floor of Sovinto in a three-room apartment, and with four kids. They were caretakers of the hall then, and I spent a lot of time with them. I practically lived at Sovinto, so I could play there with my cousins. They had to go up several flights of stairs to reach their living quarters, so I can't imagine how my aunt climbed all those stairs when she brought groceries up or when carrying one of my cousins.

I remember the giant fans that were used to circulate air in the hall. My cousin and I used to step inside of them when they were turned off, and we were lucky that no one turned the switch on or we could have been cut into pieces. I remember once when one of my cousins climbed out of an upstairs window so he could walk across a high ledge that skirted the building. My father happened to be outside and saw him there on the ledge, so he came running upstairs and pulled my cousin back in through the window. Sovinto was on the corner of West Eighth Street and Joseph Avenue. At the time it was built, it was known as the largest wooden building in America.

I once had a job picking strawberries at a farm in Geneva, and I got paid only a nickel a quart. Another time I babysat for kids for the entire summer and got paid sixty-four dollars. My mother would take one outfit and alter it into something else. Once she took a red coat and cut it down for a jacket. A seamstress made me a black-and-white checked skirt, and piping was made for the jacket from the same checked material. When I was in my teens, I wore saddle shoes with white socks, rolled-up jeans, and blouses with colored ties or scarves.

My husband, Jim Salo, and I grew up on the same street—West Ninth—so we knew each other from childhood; in fact, he was one of the kids who also played at the city dump. Jim was adopted by and grew up living with his paternal grandparents, Hedwig (Hjerpe) and John Hunnisalo (shortened to Salo), and they always spoke Finnish in the home. So when Jim first went to kindergarten, he couldn't speak English yet, and his grandmother never did learn English.

She shopped daily for meats and vegetables, and she cooked on a coal stove. Sometimes she dropped a whole fish into the pot of soup. She had an icebox, but didn't own a refrigerator until the last few years of her life.

Jim wore dungarees and penny loafers when he was in his teens, and he always wanted to own a white ski uniform like those worn by Finnish soldiers during the war with Russia in the winter of 1939.

Jim and I were married in Bethany Lutheran Church on May 8, 1954. I saved up to buy my wedding dress, which cost seventy-five dollars. It was a strapless, waltz-length, white lace dress with a net jacket. I still have it, after fifty years. And Jim still carries my wedding photo in his wallet.

After we were married for three weeks, Jim left for a seven-month world cruise with the U.S. Navy. He went to places around the globe during this tour. Meanwhile, I went to work as a secretary at the Ashtabula Telephone Company. My plan was to save as much money as I could so we could get our own place when Jim got back. I lived with my folks while he was gone, so I didn't have a lot of living expenses then, and we were able to make a down payment on a house when Jim got out of the navy.

Jim and I have three children: Tim, who was born February 29, 1956; Steve, born September 1, 1958; and Kristy, April 22, 1962. We also have one step-grandson and three step-great-grandchildren.

My mother died in 1997, and my dad lived alone until he came to live with us during the last year of his life. He died on April 12, 2005, when he was ninety-seven.

We've inherited some things from our parents and grandparents. I wear my grandmother Bihlajama's thick, gold wedding band. I also have an old family Bible, a lot of old photographs, homemade loomed rugs, a wooden potato masher, and a wooden spatula for removing bread from the oven. Jim inherited his grandmother's dining room table with claw feet and his grandfather's music stand that he used when he played with the Humina Band.

We went to Finland in 1999. Finland is such a clean, modern, advanced place, but it also has so much history and natural beauty. It was more than we expected it to be, and we hope we've instilled pride in our children for their Finnish heritage.

I think the best qualities of the Finns are their integrity, their hard-working nature, and their *sisu* [inner strength]. Their downfalls would probably be stubbornness and drunkenness.

Jim Salo is retired from the Illuminating Company. He and Marilyn make their home in Kingsville, Ohio, and they are members of Conneaut's Good Shepherd Lutheran Church.

Eugene Seline

My father's name was William Seline, and he came from Ilmajoki when he was eighteen. He had signed a contract to work three years building railroads in Montana and Wyoming; after that he went to a lumber camp in Wisconsin. In Finland our name was spelled Selin [pronounced Sell'in], but my father added an e to make it easier to pronounce [Se-leen´].

My mother, Hulda, emigrated from Seinäjoki when she was sixteen. She went to Monessen, Pennsylvania, and she found work there as a domestic. My mother married a man in Monessen who worked in a shop that made tools. He did some kind of grinding, and the stuff from the grinder settled in his lungs. So he was told he should find a different kind of job, and they moved to Wisconsin because they heard it was more like Finland up there, and that it would be better for his health. My dad rented a room from them. Then my mother's first husband died not too long after they had been in Wisconsin.

My father was a manager of this lumber camp that the railroad owned, and he supervised thirty-five other guys. They bought timber from the farmers. Then they made that wood into railroad ties. After he met my mother and they got married, she was a cook in this lumber camp. They had a bunkhouse for the men, and another log house was the cookhouse. We had a sauna there, too. My mother had to get some hired help with all that cooking and cleaning.

My sister Irene is the oldest, then my brother Clarence. I'm the youngest, born on April 19, 1914, in Clifford, Wisconsin. I was born in a log cabin. By the time I was eight years old, I was doing a man's work. I was a teamster—driving horses that hauled the logs out of the woods.

In 1924, when I was about ten, my family moved to Conneaut because my mother's sister and her family lived there. My dad didn't want to work in a factory, though; he wanted to farm, so we didn't stay in Conneaut very long. We first rented a farm south of Geneva for two years and then moved to Saybrook Township, where my dad worked a farm that was owned by a family in Cleveland. My dad also did carpentry work around that area.

I started school in Wisconsin, went on to Saybrook School, and graduated in 1932 in Conneaut. We always went to Conneaut for Christmas and other holidays like that, and we went there during summers, too. I remember one year Christmas had been a real mild day. We stayed the night, and the next day we started back and we got into a snowstorm so heavy that we had a terrible time getting home to Geneva.

I went to summer church school in Conneaut because my mother was a devout Lutheran until the day she died. My father, though, was a nonchurch Finn. He liked to go visit at the Yellow Hall, and he went to Sovinto, too. We had friends who lived at Haywood Beach, and that's where I'd go swimming in Lake Erie. I always had a bicycle, too, while I was growing up, and I used to ski in Wisconsin.

During the Depression, my dad planted big potato crops on a farm he leased on South Amboy Road (Conneaut). He'd get so many potatoes that he would give them away to people that needed some.

I first worked at a Finn dairy in Conneaut for about ten years. Then wartime came along, and General Electric in Conneaut needed people in their plant. I worked there on second shift for twelve years. When I worked that shift I had almost all day to do something else, so I studied the insurance business on the side. I worked for GE sixteen total years to get my pension rights in. And one thing I learned to do was save money.

I married Olga Sobada in the early 1930s. She was Slovenian and Scotch-Irish. We had two boys: Eugene, born in 1935; and David, born in 1944. My wife was a well-known dance teacher. She had the "Olga Seline Dance Studio" in Conneaut and Jefferson. The last place she taught was in the old Palace Ballroom in Ashtabula.

My oldest boy went to Case Institute of Technology and studied civil engineering and architecture. Then David, the younger one, was at Bowling Green University studying law. He was in his senior year when he decided to go into the air force, then he was sent to Vietnam and spent one year there. Boy, those were the two worst days of my life—when Dave was sent to Vietnam and when Olga died of cancer. She was only forty-six years old when she died in 1963.

My brother Clarence was a painting and decorating contractor, so after I retired from my insurance business, he needed my help to supervise about thirty union painters. It took all his time to figure out jobs, and he didn't have time to see if everyone was working or not. This job in Minerva [Ohio] was supposed to be for three months, but it kept me occupied for three years, and he sure paid me pretty good.

In the meantime one of my friends in Conneaut passed away. We had met through the dance studio when his girls took lessons. He left a wife with six kids and nothing to support them with. Well, I had a big four-bedroom house, so I offered to marry this widow, and they all came to live with me. We weren't married too many years, but I was still those kids' foster parent. I still keep in touch with the three girls. The oldest boy passed away, and the middle boy works out of New York City.

My oldest son worked in Germany for thirty-three years doing engineering work for the U.S. Army. When I made a trip to Finland in 1965 I was in Tampere, and my son and daughter-in-law arranged to meet me there for a visit.

At the age of ninety-one (2005), Eugene lives in his own home on Lake Road in Conneaut.

Hilda Susanna Jouppila Kohta

My mother, Hulda Ranta, was born in 1884 in Jalasjärvi, Finland. She came to this country when she was sixteen, in 1900. My mother's father first bought passage for himself, his wife, and two of their youngest children. A little while later, he sent for my mother, who was one of the older children. My mother earned a living doing housework until she met my father.

My father, Jacob Jouppila, was born in 1877 in Seinäjoki, and he didn't meet my mother until they were in America. They were married in 1906, and I was born in Cleveland on August 16, 1907. I was their only child. I don't remember too much about my early years in Cleveland except for one streetcar ride. Streetcars used to run from Cleveland to Chardon, and I remember my mother taking me on one of those and I got deathly sick. My mother took me into a drugstore where they gave me something to settle my stomach.

We moved to a farm in Huntsburg, Ohio, in 1910. I went to schools in both Huntsburg and then in Chardon. I started school in a one-room schoolhouse where all the grades from one to eight were in one room. That's where we learned our reading, writing, and arithmetic. A potbellied stove heated the school during winter, and kids who didn't behave were told to stand in a corner. My desk had an inkwell, and I had a metal lunch pail that usually had a meat sandwich and an apple in it. I walked the one-half mile to school, no matter what kind of weather we were having.

I was the only Finnish child in our neighborhood, and I'm not sure when I learned to speak English. I must have known some English when I started school because I went through two grades in one year. I played with a neighbor girl who spoke English, so I must have learned some of the language from her. We always spoke Finnish at home, though, and my mother taught me the Finnish alphabet and how to count to one hundred in Finnish. My mother never went to school, but she could still read and write. She learned how to read from her mother—my grandmother. Our food was mostly milk and potatoes, and we had a lot of homemade breads. I still bake bread occasionally.

My first job was as a babysitter for a family who lived in Fairport Harbor. I was twelve then, and a tall, good-sized girl for my age, so the family trusted me to take their children to swim in Lake Erie, even though I couldn't swim. When I was fifteen, I spent two weeks in Fairport Harbor so I could go to confirmation classes. The Lutheran minister was very strict, and all us kids were sort of afraid of him, but I learned my catechism book backward and frontward. I still have that small book. We hardly ever went to church because we didn't have the means to get into town to go to church regularly.

My parents got a divorce when I was seventeen, and I went to live with my grandparents in Chardon. I graduated from high school in Chardon in 1925. After that, I went to the Spencerian Business College, in Cleveland, for two years.

I met Toivo Kohta in Chardon; he was a neighbor who was acquainted with my cousin's family. Toivo was born in Crystal Falls, Michigan, on June 1, 1903, but his parents had emigrated from Finland. We just decided to get married, but we couldn't find a minister to marry us that day—August 2, 1930. So we finally ended up going to Cleveland and, with my cousin's help, we hunted down a Hungarian minister and he married us in his home. It wasn't like the weddings people have today. I wore an ordinary dress that I'd worked in all day, and the minister's housekeeper and my cousin were our witnesses. Most people didn't have big church weddings in those days, because they cost a lot of money.

We lived for a while in Fairport Harbor, then in Montville, and then we went to live with my father in Williamsfield Township [Ashtabula County]. When we first moved to that neighborhood, there were some people who were very much against the Finns; they seemed to think Finns had bad reputations.

We had six children: Ellen; Charles; Betty; Ruth; and the twins, Ida and Paul. We never got food stamps or anything like that during the Depression, but we had chickens and used to trade eggs for money at the A&P. At one time we had hundreds of chickens, and we sold eggs to a man who came to the house to buy eggs by the case. Toivo didn't actively serve in any war, but he was enrolled in the navy during wartime so he received a monthly pension of forty-two dollars. During the Depression, though, that was cut to six dollars a month. Of course, the cost of living was drastically cheaper than what it is today. You can't believe the price of stuff in those days. You could get five pounds of hamburger for a quarter, and Red Circle or Eight O'Clock coffee was seventeen cents a pound. We had a dairy herd, too, but we sold it off in 1941 and kept just one milk cow.

I remember, too, when some of the Finns in the community got together to send money to Finland to help them during World War II.

We had a sauna, and Saturday evening was bath night. Some of the neighbors would usually come over for a sauna, and I remember there was one woman who wanted to try the sauna. She took a bath before she came over because she wanted to be clean before she went in. We all laughed about that. She thought she was clean until she sat in the sauna, then she was horrified by what came off her skin when she sweated.

In April of 1944 we had a terrible fire. One of our neighbors, Ora Carkhuff, happened to look up the road and saw black smoke and flames coming out of our roof. I was cleaning up the kitchen after our noontime meal when I heard a banging at the door. It was Ora, all excited, telling me what she saw. I stepped outside to see for myself, then ran back inside because my twins were taking a nap in their crib. They weren't even a year old at that time. Anyway, it didn't take long before neighbors came running to help us. A couple of them grabbed the crib and wheeled it outside with the twins still in it. Some of the men went into my pantry and began handing out my canning jars full of food. Others were trying to save our furniture and take it outside. Our lunch dishes were still on the kitchen table, so a few of the men bundled up the tablecloth with the dirty dishes in it and carried it outside. By then the fire got too hot for anyone to go back in, so we just stood in the yard and watched it burn.

Later, we found out that the fire had started in the chimney and spread across the wood shingles on the roof. We eventually rebuilt the house, but it wasn't easy. For three summers and two winters, we had to live in the garage.

My father died when he was in his sixties. He had worked in a copper mine in Michigan when he was young, and he also smoked cigarettes. He was also so sick during the 1918 flu epidemic, it's a miracle he even survived.

Toivo and I celebrated our forty-ninth wedding anniversary on August 2, 1979. Then he died four days later. He was seventy-six then. My mother lived to be ninety-seven, so maybe I inherited my long life from her. My hearing and eyesight aren't very good, and I walk with a cane, but I'm all right, otherwise.

My daughter, Ellen, and I traveled to Finland in 1987. We visited relatives in Seinäjoki and I celebrated my eightieth birthday there. Ellen can speak a little Finnish and is the one most interested in family history and memories. When I talked to people in Finland, they told me I spoke words that people used one hundred years ago, but weren't used any longer. I used to speak Finnish quite often with a neighbor lady who was also Finnish, but after she died I didn't speak it much anymore. It's odd how you remember some things and not others.

At age ninety-eight (2005), Hilda still lives alone in her farmhouse. Her son, Charles, who lives nearby, visits daily and does her errands. Her youngest daughter, Ida, also visits and drives her mother to doctor's appointments. Hilda has twelve living grandchildren. One grandson died in an auto accident, and another grandson and a granddaughter died at birth. In addition, Hilda has nine great-grandchildren, three step-great-grandchildren, and one step-great-great-grandchild.

Ina Maria Peaspanen Bloom

Ina's father, Kalle Piispanen (anglicized to Peaspanen), emigrated from Saarijärvi, Finland, in 1901, and settled in Monessen, Pennsylvania. Ina's mother, Wilhelmina (Wilma) Pirttinen, emigrated from Karstula, Finland, and also settled in Monessen around the same time as Kalle. Wilma was sixteen when she arrived and eighteen when she married twenty-five-year-old Kalle in 1903.

Over the following years, the Peaspanens had eight children: Leonard, Eino, Urho, Aune, Ina (born on February 20, 1911, in Brownsville, Pennsylvania), Elmer, David, and William. During the week that Ina was born, Urho, who was four, and Aune, who was two, both died from "black fever," an acute infection with high temperature and dark-red skin lesions. In that same week there was a measles epidemic and the Monongahela River had overflowed its banks. All the children were baptized in the Monessen Lutheran Church.

The family next lived on a farm east of Charleroi, Pennsylvania, near the Monongahela River. Kalle worked in the nearby coal mines, leaving Wilma and the two oldest boys to do the farm work. The boys had a small coal mine of their own, dug out of a hillside, and this coal was used in the upstairs and downstairs fireplaces, as well as in the kitchen cookstove. In addition to the farmwork and housework, Wilma managed the finances; yet, she was remembered as one who laughed and sang a lot in the home.

When Leonard and Eino were sixteen and fourteen, respectively, their parents didn't want them working in the coal mines so the family moved to a Jefferson, Ohio, farm on Doyle Road.

In 1929, Ina graduated from the Grand River Institute, Austinburg, Ohio, where she had studied college-preparatory courses. After graduation, she then took a short business course, yet she was unable to work outside the home because she was needed to assist on their large farm. An additional course taken in home nursing, however, provided her with the skills needed to care for her mother, who was stricken with cancer. Wilma was bedridden for nineteen months before dying at the age of fifty.

Ina met George Walter (Wally) Bloom, from Ashtabula Harbor, when they were both seventeen. Wally was a son of Finnish immigrants whose surname was initially Hegblum, but it was anglicized to Bloom, possibly at the time of their emigration from Finland. Wally was a member of Zion Lutheran Church. He also played trombone in the Harbor High School Band. Because of Ina's heavy family responsibilities on the farm, she didn't marry Wally until September 9, 1933, five years after they met.

During World War II, Wally was drafted into the navy when their three older children were all under ten years of age. Their four children are Patricia Maxine, born in 1934; James Walter, 1938; Janis Ann, 1944; and Ruth Ina, 1946. Both before and after the war, Wally worked with Ina's family on their dairy farm and then in his own family's furnace business and as an ironworker.

The Blooms then bought a small farm on Chapel Road, Plymouth Township, where they taught homemaking and animal/farming skills to 4-H groups over a sixty-year period. As 4-H leaders, they were involved with the Ashtabula County Fairs and the fair board. They were also active in the Austinburg Grange, and both were members and officers of Bethany Lutheran Church. Other memberships were in Eastern Star and the Masons. The family hobby was riding and showing quarter horses, so they were members of the Dusty Boots Riding Club.

Ina did not work outside the home until her youngest daughter, Ruth, was a junior in high school. In 1963 she was employed at the Commercial Bank in Ashtabula, followed by an executive secretarial position at the Ashtabula Area Development Association (Citizens in Action), beginning in 1966. The association dissolved in June 1990, but Ina continued to help with the "Blessing of the Fleet" ceremonies.

Ina's involvement and service to Bethany Lutheran was extensive. She became a member of Bethany Sisters (Women of Bethany) at age eighteen, and she sang in the chancel choir throughout her years. She taught Sunday school and vacation Bible school. She was a member and officer of the Mother-Teacher Guild and served as a "Friendly Visitor." Ina learned to read and write Finnish from her parents when they asked her to correspond with relatives in Finland. This practice enabled her to write the church's council minutes in both English and Finnish and read minutes in both languages at council meetings. [By the mid- to late-fifties, only English was required.] She served as council secretary for many years and was on the council for one term.

During World War II, Ina sent coffee and other supplies to relatives in Finland, and continued to maintain communication and initiate visitations in both Finland and the United States with her parents' families.

All their children were grown when Wally died of a heart attack in January 1977, at age sixty-five. Ina continued living in their farmhouse.

Along with other church women, one of Ina's favorite church activities was making *nisua* for bake sales. She taught her children and grandchildren to make this cardamom-flavored coffee bread, too, but she used the same recipe as in the church kitchen that yielded so many loaves that she was able to share them with her brothers' families.

Ina played the piano and organ "by ear" and often shared these talents with residents at local nursing homes. She also volunteered to drive family or friends to the grocery store or for medical and dental appointments. She kept active by bowling with her Grange team, twice a week, from fall to spring each year. Her love, encouragement, and support for her family were unflagging. Her enthusiasm for life and friendly smile were further testaments of her Christian faith.

Along with heart complications, she suffered a stroke in the last year of her life. Ina Bloom died on October 17, 1991, at the age of eighty. In addition to her four children, she was survived by twelve grandchildren, eighteen great-grandchildren, and three great-great-grandchildren. Her only son, James Bloom, died in April 2004 of cancer.

Janis Bloom Eldridge contributed these accounts of her mother's life.

Oliver Kaura

My father, Victor Kaura, left Peräseinäjoki, Finland, for economic reasons. He arrived in Ashtabula in 1901 because he had friends there. My mother, Minnie Sippola, came from Ylistaro in 1903 when she was twelve years old. Both families had friends here and chose to come as things weren't very good economically in Finland. My mother and father met in Ashtabula and were married in Bethany Lutheran Church.

My father was a carpenter, and my mother worked at the dry-cleaning place on Joseph Avenue. I remember she would wave to me out of the window when I came home from school. I was born on August 7, 1912, when they lived on Bridge Street. I grew up on Bridge Street and went to Washington Elementary School. I didn't have any brothers or sisters, just cousins. My father had a brother and sister here, and my mother had three sisters in Ashtabula.

My father was a carpenter, and he built our first house on Ohio Avenue, so I went to school at the Jackson building for one year. Then he built another house on West Fourteenth Street, and that's where we lived the rest of my growing-up years.

My father played first-chair clarinet in the Humina [Murmur] Band and some other relatives played in the band, too. I played trumpet with the band, and when they went on their Finland tour in 1927 I wanted to go along, but my father wouldn't permit me to go because I wasn't quite fifteen at the time.

I joined the Keefer-Smith Orchestra in Erie while I was still in high school, and that's when I joined the musicians' union. I played for other dances when they didn't interfere with the Erie band's schedule, which was every Saturday night and on holidays. It was my first paying job.

After my 1930 high school graduation, I played with different bands and was earning twenty-five dollars a night—more than my father was earning at that time. I first joined Markko and the Californians. Two of us guys were the only ones who weren't from California. Then I joined with a Southern band and played all over: New Orleans, Florida, and one summer we played by a lake in New Jersey. They had the blue laws in effect there, and we couldn't have any jobs on Sunday, so when we got done at midnight one Saturday night several of us went to New York which was about thirty-five miles away. So then I stayed in New York and started to play there at different clubs and with different bands. In fact, I played at the Roxy Theatre. I spent twelve years in New York, from 1933 to 1945. I played with bands while studying at Julliard to become a classical cellist.

Then the war broke out. Guys were drafted or enlisted and bands began to break up. I had four weeks of training at Great Lakes Naval Center in Illinois, but by then the war was over and I didn't have to serve.

In 1945 I came back to Ashtabula and was staying with my parents when Charlie Potti came to see me. He said, "Let's go to a Scandinavian party in Cleveland." It was a Saturday night, so I said, "Okay, I'll go with you." On the way back, on the east side of Geneva, we were hit head-on by a semi, and I wound up in the hospital. I have a scar right there yet, and it tore my lip up inside and tore my muscles there.

Kaarlo Mackey and Ward Hamm came to see me in the hospital. "Well," they said, "Oliver, you'll never play professionally again, so you might as well join us and teach in the schools." So I helped Kaarlo, who was the band director in Conneaut schools—part time—from 1947 to 1956, and the other half of my time, during those years, I spent with Ward Hamm, who was the band director at Ashtabula High. Then there was a full-time opening at Harbor High School for a director, and I was hired there in 1957. I continued there for twenty-five years.

I attended Kent State University, the Cleveland Institute of Music, and Case Western Reserve University. I received my bachelor's degree in 1957 and my master's degree in 1959, both from Kent. In addition to my high-school duties, I was a part-time instructor at the Kent campuses in Trumbull, Geauga, and Ashtabula Counties. I enjoyed the challenge of teaching university students. My teaching courses included Music Fundamentals, Music Appreciation, General Music for Classroom Teachers, and America's Music. I retired from my Kent classes at the end of the fall semester in 1984.

I also directed the chancel choir at Bethany Lutheran Church for twenty-five years: 1960 to 1985. In 1972 I toured Germany with the Harbor High band. Seventy students went, and we played all over in Amsterdam and in Berlin. Fourteen bands paraded on the Kurfürstendamm in Berlin while an estimated fifty thousand spectators lined the street. Then we went across Check Point Charlie into East Germany on a bus. That was, of course, still under Russia's Communist rule. After twenty-five years of directing at Harbor High, I retired in 1982.

I met my wife, Katherine (Kathy) Swoboda, when she was a student at Kent-Ashtabula in my Music of Fundamentals class. Kathy and her mother had emigrated from Germany in 1951 and settled in Pittsburgh where Kathy went to school. After she graduated from high school in 1958, she and her mother moved to Ashtabula because Kathy's mother met and married a man from Ashtabula. I married Kathy in 1960, and we have one daughter, Suzanne, who was born in 1962. Kathy earned her degree and became an instructor of German at Kent-Ashtabula and also taught German in the public schools.

After Oliver's retirement, he continued to give private lessons and was often called upon to judge solo and ensemble contests. In 1982, he and a group of string musicians met to play together, then wind and brass musicians joined them, and soon the Ashtabula Chamber Orchestra was formed. The orchestra still performs, and is known as the Ashtabula Area Orchestra, in residence at Kent State University's Ashtabula campus.

After his time-honored, laudable musical career, Oliver Kaura died in his home of a lingering illness at the age of eighty-nine on February 8, 2001. He is survived by his wife, his daughter, and two grandsons, Jacob and Andrew Mayer.

Mamie Taanila Luoma

Mamie's father, Daniel Taanila, was born in Nivela, Finland, on October 25, 1880. He was baptized and confirmed as a Lutheran. Daniel emigrated from Finland on March 30, 1902, when he was twenty-two, going first to Monessen, Pennsylvania, where other Finns had already settled to work in the coal mines and mills in that area.

Mamie's mother, Saima Emilia Johanson, was born in Jalasjärvi, Finland, on June 8, 1879, and was also baptized and confirmed as a Lutheran. She arrived in Monessen in June of 1901 and most likely met Daniel in the Lutheran church. Saima and Daniel were married in Monessen on December 30, 1904, and lived first in rented rooms above a temperance hall.

Daniel earned a living by driving a bakery-delivery wagon, and their first child, Martha Elisabeth, was born in Monessen on March 9, 1906.

The Taanilas moved to Ashtabula Harbor in 1907, and here eight more children were born to them: Maria Ester Irene on April 7, 1908; Meimi (Mamie) Eleanora on November 19, 1909; Eeva Mathilda was born on February 7, 1911, and died eleven days later. Twins were born next: Mirjam Ethel and Toivo Johannes on October 18, 1912, but Toivo died three weeks later. Following the twins were Maila Ellida Isebell (Isabel), born on January 20, 1914; Magda Hagar, September 6, 1916; and John Martin Waldemar, November 18, 1920. The seven surviving children were all baptized and confirmed in the first Bethany Lutheran Church where, over the years, Daniel sang in the choir, taught Sunday school, served on the church council, was a lay speaker, and was at one time president of the church.

Daniel's faith was carried out in their home, as well. Mamie recalled the great influenza epidemic in 1918 when her mother was ill: "Mother almost died, then father prayed, and she recovered. Without prayer, I don't think she would have survived."

Although Daniel attended Christmas Eve church services, Saima kept the children home during these evening services. Since there were so many lighted candles, she felt her children might be endangered if a fire were to break out. Saima, like most women at that time, baked all their bread, and *lihaperunoita* [meat stew] often bubbled on the stove.

The Taanila family home was on Erie Street [upper West Eighth Street], and Daniel worked as a car inspector for the New York Central System and eventually retired from there. The family went to Turva Hall only when the church was represented, but they were never permitted to go to Sovinto Hall, because dances were held there and dancing did not meet with Daniel's approval. When the Humina Band held outdoor concerts, Mamie went to listen with her older sisters, but she was frightened by the band's loudness and clung to her sister Martha until she became more accustomed to the sounds.

Mamie graduated in 1927 from Harbor High School, and her first job was clerking at Neisner's, a five- and ten-cent store on Main Street, where two of her sisters had also worked.

On May 24, 1930, Mamie married William Luoma in Bethany's parsonage. William was born in Monessen, Pennsylvania, in 1909, the son of Kristo Luoma and Elizabeth Pykari Luoma. The newlyweds lived on Joseph Avenue during the Depression but didn't need any assistance because Bill had saved enough money to carry them through. Three children were born to the couple: Melodie, born in 1931; William, in 1934; and Virginia, in 1936. Bill worked at the Ashtabula Bow Socket, a manufacturing plant.

After receiving organ lessons from Mildred Nelson, who was organist at an Ashtabula Swedish church, Mamie became assistant to Bethany's organist, Franz Holmstrom, in 1929 when she was nineteen. Holmstrom was also the "cantor" in the old Bethany church, or one who leads the congregation in singing the liturgy and hymns, a custom carried over from the churches in Finland. During the years Mamie performed as an assistant, Holmstrom gave her no forewarning when he wanted her to take over; he simply tapped her on the shoulder and whispered, "*Tuu soitamaa*" [Come play]. When

Holmstrom stepped aside after being organist for forty-five years, Mamie began her long career as full-time organist in 1945. In addition to the Sunday services and added Lenten and Advent services, Mamie also played for weddings and funerals. When the new Michigan Avenue Bethany Church was officially dedicated on October 2, 1955, Mamie walked from her home to practice, almost daily, on the large Pels pipe organ.

Yet Mamie's dedication as an organist wasn't her only contribution to the church. For forty-five years, she was a church-school teacher and superintendent, a confirmation instructor, and helped reorganize the church school's curriculum from Finnish into English in 1942. She was director and accompanist of the Mother Choir from 1943 to 1972, the Finnish-singing group founded in 1940 by her sister, Isabel Maki.

Isabel married the Reverend Otto Maki on June 20, 1939. Maki pastored Bethany's congregation from 1935 to 1943. During his eight-year tenure, he successfully began using English, instead of Finnish alone, in the services, and expanded the use of English in the Sunday school. Under his leadership, lots were purchased for Bethany's future building site, and the first Camp Luther was purchased on Lake Road East. Pastor Maki and Isabel left Ashtabula for Michigan in 1943, and in the following years Isabel served capably as a pastor's wife wherever they were called.

Mamie also organized a quilting workshop in 1968 where church women gathered to sew; subsequently, they supplied the Lutheran World Relief agency with about one hundred quilts annually. Moreover, Mamie was instrumental in developing two books—*What the Bible Says* and *Tune in to God*—that were used by the Women of Bethany as Bible study guides.

Serving the church became an important part of the lives of the next generation. Mamie's son William received his bachelor of divinity degree in 1960 and went on to serve as a Lutheran pastor in Port Clinton, Logan, and Bowling Green—all in Ohio. Daughter Melodie sang in Bethany's Chancel Choir as well as gave vocal solo performances. Melodie also led the Children's Choir, and directed the Women's Ensemble, a small choral group organized in December of 1965. In 1974, this group performed at Wittenberg University for a convention of Lutheran Church Women and recorded an album, "The Ensemble Sings," that included Christmas songs and other sacred and secular music. In addition, Melodie volunteered as director of Christian education in 1964 and then became a paid staff member in 1974, a position she held until her retirement in the early 1990s.

Sunday, May 27, 1984, was declared Mamie Luoma Day at Bethany. She was honored for her long years of service, along with other past and present musicians, and so ended her fifty-five-year career as church organist.

Her mother, Saima, died in 1965, at the age of eighty-six, and her father Daniel passed away in 1967, at eighty-seven. After sixty-five years of marriage, Mamie's husband, William, died on August 18, 1995. Mamie's final days were spent at the Ashtabula County Nursing Home, in Kingsville, Ohio. With family longevity in her favor, she lived until ninety-two, dying on November 26, 2001. Survivors were her three children, five grandchildren, ten great-grandchildren, and two of her sisters.

Although Mamie was interviewed during her last years in the nursing home, additional research with church records revealed many other factors of her and her family's contributions to Bethany Lutheran Church and are included here.

Maire (Myra) Suleima Wahlstrom

My mother's parents, Peter and Miriam Heikkinen, were the first to come to this country from Finland. They first settled in Minnesota, but my grandfather didn't care for farming in that area, so they moved to Hancock, Michigan, where he found work in the copper mines. They had two daughters born there: Katri (Kate), in 1878; and Hilma Aliina , my mother, in 1885. My mother was only twelve when her mother died and thirteen when her father died. My aunt Kate was seven years older than my mother, so she must have been able to make a home for her.

My father, George Einar Wahlstrom, was born in Helsinki, Finland, April 22, 1883. His father had a cobbler's shop, and my father had one brother, Uno, and a sister, Eli. Eli's daughter's name was Maire and she died when she was only five, so my father named me after Maire. My aunt Eli had a gift shop in Helsinki until she was about seventy-five years old. She sent us Christmas gifts every year, and we especially liked the fantastic books where the pictures popped up when you turned the page.

My father came to this country in 1902, but before that he had a good education. He went to the public schools and then spent six years at Helsinki's military band school. He studied theory and harmony there. Then he went to Berlin where he took a course in orchestration and conducting at the

Brandenburg Conservatory. He also had voice lessons in Helsinki from one of Finland's greatest baritones.

When my dad came here in 1902, he first organized a band in Maynard, Massachusetts. In 1905 he was a conductor of Monessen's Louhi Band. Then, in 1906, he came to Conneaut to conduct the Pohjan Aalto Band.

When my dad went to Calumet, Michigan, in 1907, to conduct the *Humu* Band, that's when he met my mother. Calumet is just north of Hancock, where she was then living. They were married in 1908, and their first daughter, Irma Cecilia, was born there August 30, 1909. My dad conducted a military band in Red Lodge, Montana, that same year, but I don't know if my mother went with him or not. Anyway, in 1910 he spent a year in Berlin for postgraduate studies; then he went back to Michigan, where he conducted a band in Ishpeming and directed the Sointu mixed chorus in Calumet. A second daughter, my sister, Georgia Marie, was born August 25, 1913. They moved to Monessen in 1915. My dad conducted the Louhi Band there, and that's where the three youngest daughters were born: Kirsten (Charlotte), August 29, 1915; then me—Myra—on April 3, 1917. Our youngest sister, Airi Elli Katri, was born on July 30, 1920. My dad took the Monessen band on a concert tour to New York City in 1918 and to Finland in 1920.

My mother probably was upset when my dad got the letter that offered him another conducting job in Ashtabula Harbor, because they had moved so many times. I remember I went on the train with my father to Ashtabula when he first had a meeting scheduled there. I was five and it was my first train ride. I was fascinated with the train, and even more with the paper cups we had to drink with from the water cooler. My dad was very patient with me. When we got there, he took me to someone's house on West Eighth Street, and for some reason this lady wasn't very nice to me. She put me in a closet, and I don't know why she did, because I wasn't crying. Then I went to stay with the Koykka family, who had a daughter, Ari, my same age. Ari and I became lifelong friends.

The whole family moved to Ashtabula in the mid-summer of 1922, after Dr. Wenner, superintendent of the Harbor Special Schools, hired my dad. He was to direct the Humina Band, and he also organized and directed both instrumental and vocal music at the Harbor schools. He gave private lessons, too, and started school bands in Andover and Kingsville. He was always hopping around to band practices. He loved it!

We first rented a house on West Eighth Street that was owned by the Collanders, and the first house my dad bought was on West Third Street. I grew up in the Harbor and went to Washington, Jackson, and Harbor High School. We belonged to Bethany Lutheran when my father directed the choir there. When my father started to direct the choir at the First Presbyterian Church, we went there.

We celebrated Christmas and every Finnish holiday. My mother made traditional Finnish dishes and she baked *nisua* every Friday and baked bread every Saturday. I used to go to the store with my little wagon to get the big bags of flour for her. We had three meals a day together, and those mealtimes were the happiest memories of my childhood. Father told us stories that were mostly happy ones. We sat down at the same time, and he never forgot to thank Mother for the meals. He was a gentleman, but could be quite a disciplinarian, too. When we talked about him years later, someone asked, "Weren't you afraid of Father?" I said, "No," because he was a pushover, and was very gentle and sweet at home with his children. He loved all the kids he taught, and their families, too.

I remember Sovinto Hall because I spent a lot of time there. They had plays and dances and holiday banquets, and I always went with my father. There was a small building behind Sovinto where they had band practices. Father had a lot of Italian friends, too, because he spoke Italian, English, Finnish, Swedish, and German.

We went every Sunday when the band played a concert or for picnics. The Humina band members pampered and babied me. I guess I was a little gold digger, because they gave me lots of quarters, dimes, and nickels. I bought my first little red coat with chinchilla trim and a tam with the money they gave me.

When I was in the sixth grade, the school band went to class A competition. I played the last chair in the cornet section. Afterward, the judge said to my father that he had never seen such a little cornet player in all his life. Father stuck his chest out and I knew he was very proud of me. We had a wonderful father.

When my dad died, that was the greatest tragedy because it happened so suddenly. He had surgery for a ruptured appendix on August 18, 1930, at Ashtabula General Hospital. They thought the surgery was successful, but then he had complications and they did a second operation four days later. Then five days after that, on the twenty-fifth, he died. He was only forty-seven. The newspaper had his picture and a long story about him, and a lot of people went to his funeral. Some came from as far away as Monessen. He was buried in Edgewood Cemetery. I was only thirteen then, and it took me a long time to cope with his death. It was very hard because we all depended a lot on him. I just muddled through life after that for a while.

When my father died, it was during the Depression, so we lost the house and everything. When I was fifteen, I went to live with my sister, Irma Stenroos, and her family. Her children, George and Leta, thought of me as their sister instead of an aunt. While I was still in high school I worked in the old Turner's Drug Store on Bridge Street. After I graduated in 1935 I still worked for Turner's in their new Lake Avenue location.

Then, in 1939, I moved to Cleveland. I worked for General Electric throughout the World War II years. By 1952 I became the distribution manager for Sherwin Williams Company, and they then transferred me to California. My mother came to live with me in California when she was seventy-five years old. She died in 1965 when she was eighty, and she's buried in Inglewood, California. I got transferred once more, in 1970, to Oakland, California, where the Sherwin Williams regional office was located.

I left California when I was seventy-three and returned to Ashtabula Harbor, in 1990, where I found an apartment on West Sixth Street. That's just a few blocks from where my family lived together the last time.

Myra was honored on two occasions during her later years. In May of 1996 the Finnish-American Heritage Association held a fund-raising concert at Bethany Lutheran Church. The concert was a tribute to Finland's famed composer, Jean Sibelius, and to noted musician and conductor, George Wahlstrom. Among the three hundred in attendance was Myra Wahlstrom who was recognized as the only living daughter of George Wahlstrom.

Myra's nieces and nephews arrived from California, Michigan, New Jersey, New York, and Ohio to host Myra's eightieth birthday party. More than sixty guests were in attendance at the East Ashtabula Club's hall. She received more than one hundred cards, letters, and floral arrangements from those unable to attend. This joyful occasion proved timely, for Myra died the following year on March 15, 1998.

Allan Raymond (Ray) Keskinen

My father, Teofiilius (shortened to Filius) Keskinen, was born in Aluvus, Finland, on September 16, 1883. He landed in Boston on May 20, 1903, when he was twenty. Then he went on to Crystal Falls, Michigan, where he worked in an iron-ore mine. In April 1907 he moved to Ashtabula, Ohio.

My mother's name was Anna Wilhemiina Rantanen. Her last name was shortened to Ranta in this country. She was born on February 26, 1886, in Saarijärvi, Finland. She left there when she was twenty-one and arrived in the United States on June 24, 1907. My parents met in Ashtabula and were married there on September 25, 1908.

I was born on July 15, 1911, when they lived on York Street [West Twenty-ninth Street] in the Forty Acres region. [This area is bounded on the south by the New York Central Railroad (now Norfolk & Southern), on the west and north by the Pennsylvania Railroad (now Conrail), and on the east by the "gulf," the ravine through which the Ashtabula River winds its way to Lake Erie.] They later bought a house on Wade Street and lived there until 1923. I had a brother, Benhard, who was born in 1913; and two sisters, Kaarina, born in 1915, and Kerttu, in 1919. Our family belonged to the first Bethany Evangelical Lutheran Church on Joseph Avenue, and we went to many activities at Sovinto Hall. I can remember the dry-goods store in the Harbor that was owned by Kalle Potti, who was vice consul to Finland at the time.

My friends and I used to enjoy hunting frogs with our slingshots. Then we'd give the frogs to some of our Italian neighbors who liked to cook and eat frog legs. We used to swim, too, at different beaches along Lake Erie.

My father had visited Finland in 1905 and in 1914. Then he wanted to go and stay there in 1923, so he took all of us with him. We didn't stay, though, and returned that same year. But on our way back, when we were in Southampton, England, vaccinations were required. My dad almost died from his vaccination because infection set in. Then once we got back to Ashtabula, we had to stay with the Lahnanen family on Spruce Street [West Third Street] while my dad went looking for a house. After looking for about a month, he found a house to buy on Mary Street [West Twenty-fourth Street].

We had some relatives in Canada, and there was one who made violins. I once got a violin as a gift and my mother sent me for lessons. I had been taking lessons for about a year when I overheard my teacher say, "I've got to teach that guy, but he'll never be a musician."

During the Depression, my dad was laid off as a railroad-car repairman. Off and on, he would get calls to come back to work. Finally he was hired at the McKinnon Iron Works, and he stayed working there until he died at sixty-five on December 17, 1948. My father wrote a lot of poems in Finnish. I've had many of them translated and typed.

I graduated from Ashtabula High School in 1929. Pete Rasmus was an Ashtabula Harbor Finn who was also an Olympic-champion discus thrower.

Pete had gone to Ohio State University, and he convinced my father to send me there. So I started my studies at Ohio State in the fall of 1929, and I had fifty dollars in a checking account in a Columbus bank. Then the stock market crashed that October and the Great Depression began. When they ordered the banks to be closed, I couldn't get my money out. My dad talked to Oliver Topky [an Ashtabula marine-hardware merchant], and he gave me the money so I could go on with my studies. To buy food, I got a job in a little restaurant.

When I was at Ohio State, I had two friends who were amateur radio operators, and I got interested in it, too. I finally got my radio license and I've continued my "ham hobby" all these years.

I got my electrical engineering degree in 1933, but since the Depression was still on, I had trouble finding a job. I did some surveying work for a school and for a small airport. Then I talked to a local manufacturing guy who told me to apply at Erie Resistor in Erie, Pennsylvania. They had already turned me down, but as I was on my way out, the chief engineer happened to come by. He asked me where I had gone to school. When I told him Ohio State, the chief invited me into his office for an interview, and then he hired me. So then I worked as his assistant and as a draftsman until 1939.

I married Aina Hakundy on July 3, 1937, in the old Bethany Evangelical Lutheran Church in Ashtabula Harbor, and we first lived in Erie. Then I got a civil service job in Washington, D.C. I was an inspector of steel bakery equipment, then an inspector of steel office desks. I was sent next to Rhode Island, and then to York, Pennsylvania, to inspect welded chairs. I didn't care much for these inspection jobs, but I didn't dare quit because the war was on. After about a year, I went to work as a radar engineer for Bendix Radio in Towson, Maryland. That's where our daughter Karen was born.

When World War II ended, my family moved in with my in-laws on West Thirteenth Street in Ashtabula, and I started looking for work in Cleveland. I found a government job where we made high-quality radio antennas. They required a special wire that cost extra money to produce, but, because federal price controls were still in effect, the company couldn't charge more for them, so that job ended. Our second child, David, was born in Ashtabula in 1946.

We moved to Conneaut in 1947 when I was hired by the Astatic Corporation as an engineer. In 1953 I passed the State of Ohio engineers' exam and got my professional engineer's license. Then I was promoted to chief engineer of electronics, and I held that position until I retired in 1975.

I served on the building committee for Conneaut's Good Shepherd Lutheran Church—the one that replaced the old Finnish Lutheran Church.

Initial plans called for an electronic organ to be installed, but I convinced the committee that a pipe organ would be more appropriate for the new church. Kujala and Koski were the architects for the church, so Ray Koski drafted plans for an additional eight feet to accommodate a pipe-organ chamber after they approved my plans. Once the building got underway, I volunteered to knock out the bricks to make way for the addition. Then I supervised the construction and installation of the organ grilles that Koski had drafted, and I installed the audio system. When it came time to look for a pipe organ, I was a member of the organ search committee. Aina and I have been members of the old Lutheran Church and Good Shepherd Lutheran for sixty-eight years, and we've also been married sixty-eight years.

At age ninety-four, Ray uses his computer to communicate with cousins in Finland. He has continued his hobby of amateur radio operating and has taken the Federal Communications Commission exam to receive his commercial broadcast license.

Laina Kahelin Dieffenbacher

My mother was Hilda Maria Jokila, and she came to this country from Kauhava, Finland, in 1904, when she was seventeen. She had a friend in that same village who was going to America, too, and this friend had two small children. My mother carried one in order to not have to pay the extra fare on the boat. They were in the cheapest part of the boat, and it was pretty bad. They first landed in Quebec, and then the boat came on to New York, and then they came through Ellis Island. I have the trunk that my mother brought from Finland. My mother went to Conneaut because she had an older sister already there. Her sister's name was Adolfiina, but we called her "Fiina."

My father, Einar Kahelin, left Viitasaari in 1907 to come to America. He actually went to Hibbing, Minnesota, at first, because he had a brother there who worked in the iron mines. He didn't stay there hardly at all, because he heard about the jobs on the Great Lakes down here. So my folks met in Conneaut and were married there on April 10, 1910.

Then my father heard they were building railroad cars in Ashtabula, so they moved there and he went to work with the New York Central Railroad. Mother had boarders at home and worked pretty hard. There was lots of men who came from Finland who were either single, or were married but didn't bring their families until they earned enough money. So she had different boarders—off and on.

This house was on the corner of West Avenue and West Thirty-eighth Street, and that's where I was born, on February 7, 1911. My three brothers were born after: Toivo Henry, John Einar, and Edward William.

We had a lot of kids around when we lived in town. We played in the mud and sand, and when it rained there was ditches for the water to run down, and we couldn't wait to play in that rain and get all muddied up and have fun. We did sled-riding in the winter, and in the summer there was a Mr. Beckman, and he had a big seven-passenger touring car that took us to Highland Beach. I don't know how we reached him, but he would come and pick us up when he knew we were going. We'd go down there for a picnic, and he'd bring us back home that same day.

When we had all those boarders, why, they delivered groceries to our home. My mother would call the grocery store in the morning, and she'd have what she needed for supper for the gang. They also had a meat man who came around a little later in the day. We didn't have any preservation, but a tiny little icebox to keep milk in. The milk came in bottles, and we tried to keep that cold. Then there was a fruit and vegetable peddler that came around every other day—well, at least three times a week. We didn't have to run around for food very much; it was delivered.

I used to wash and dry dishes when we had the boarders, and I told Mother when I was grown up I'd like to get a job washing dishes, when I could get paid for it.

Transportation was a problem to get to Sunday school in the Harbor, so we rented Messiah Lutheran Church on Hiawatha Avenue for a Sunday afternoon. We had forty people there most of the time, plus the teachers.

Then we moved to the farm on North Bend Road—west of town, and between the tracks and Route 45. It was a very nice place. Now it has a painting on the barn that says "Sundance Ranch." That's where I grew up; I have very fond memories of my childhood there. We had a Finnish sauna and had coffee time. It was heated on Wednesdays and Saturdays, and a houseful of people would come there to use the sauna, and we had coffee and all the good stuff. My mother loved to entertain. We had like six or eight guests every Wednesday and Saturday.

My mother made Finn foods like *lipeakala* [lye-soaked cod], for one, and rutabaga soufflé—I loved that. And she made *nisua* and her own bread—whole wheat or rye. She baked every week, and made enough to last the week. That was a regular ritual. She used to make head cheese when they butchered animals, and it was good.

My folks didn't attend any halls. I can remember certain people came to our home asking for donations when they were building what they called the Yellow Hall. My parents did not give to it. It was called a Socialist hall, and that's all I know about it. They had dances and plays for activities in the halls, and a lot of my friends went there. I never attended anything there—no! I was grown up before I ever went to Sovinto Hall. We didn't have transportation to get around to those places when I was growing up. I did attend our church picnic grounds, called *oriva metsa* [squirrel woods]. I can remember they had big outdoor fires, and they had wash-boilers full of meat and potatoes cooking outside. I heard the Humina Band once in a while, and I remember Mr. Wahlstrom; in fact, he was our choir director at our church for a while. He was a good director.

We had a horse that we could hitch to a small buggy to get to the stores; it just had one seat in it, you know. The horse couldn't stand to go on the road that had streetcars on them. He would stand on his hind legs as soon as he would approach a streetcar. He was hard to handle. My mother and I would go shopping, and we'd take the back roads to get to the Harbor. Usually around West Sixth Street, or so, we'd tie the horse to a telephone pole there. Then we could go to the bank (there was Finnish people there in the bank), and Kuivinen's Dry Goods Store, and Felt's Shoe Store, and Brant's Meat Market.

I remember that we didn't get to go to Bethany Church very often on Sundays because we didn't have a car for the first few years. I remember going to special events at Bethany. They had a horse barn where you could park your horse and wagon. The first minister I can remember was Mannerkorpi, and I can't remember who followed him. I think it was John Saarinen, if I'm not mistaken.

I rode to school the first eight grades in a kid hack. It was like a covered wagon with this canvas over the top, and we had seats along the sides. It was pulled by three or four horses.

We had our first car in 1921 when there was still dirt roads. There wasn't school buses, and I went to high school without buses. My father worked at the railroad-car shop which was a mile away from the streetcar line. I would go as far as his shop, and then walk to the streetcar line, and then take the streetcar to the high school. There were times when cars couldn't even travel on North Bend Road, because it was so bad, so I walked. I don't think I ever missed a day in high school.

I used to pick fruit as a youngster. I made five cents a quart for picking strawberries. For the family, I picked lots of blackberries, raspberries, gooseberries, and currants. We had them on the farm, and I had to do that. I had to hoe corn and the garden. I loved gardening.

Our father lost his job on the railroad during the Depression. Because our farm was small, you couldn't make a living off of it. We had our own crops, and my father cut wood to burn in the furnace. But we helped a lot of other people. When we butchered animals, we'd always share it with our relatives or friends that didn't have any work. Everybody was poor, so we didn't even think about it.

I started in nurses' training in 1929, and it was right after that that everything started going down hill. We didn't have any money, but no one else had any money either, so we just got by without it. In December of 1931, I got through nurses' training, but there were very few nurses' jobs available. The hospitals only hired supervisors as RNs, and the rest of them were students. We did everything when we were in training, and the pay was very little. When I got through training, nurses were getting three dollars for eight-hours' work, so I went to Cleveland. I had a cousin who was a good friend of a doctor there, and I got a few private-duty cases while there. That was in the winter, and in the summer I came home to help on the farm. Then about 1932 or '33, I really got a good job in Cleveland doing housework for a family. I worked there six or eight months. Then a friend in Ashtabula got sick. She had a gall bladder operation and wanted me to come and take care of her, and so I did. Then I gradually started getting more work. Around that time I met my husband. I had met him before while I was still in nurses' training, but we just went together off and on, not steady. I knew him about four years before we were married; in fact, I knew him in school, but he was way older than I. He was seven years older.

I married Ted Dieffenbacher in December 1934. He worked for the New York Central Railroad in different positions over the years. We first had three girls—Carolyn, Mary, and Nancy—and then three boys—Theodore (Ted) and the twins, Paul and David. When we first got married, we lived in a small, brick bungalow, which I liked very much. When I was expecting our third child, we didn't have enough room, so we moved to Woodman Avenue in 1940, and Nancy was born there a few weeks after we moved. I did private-duty nursing, until 1938, for people who were sick at home.

I didn't work during World War II, but after the war there was a tremendous shortage of nurses, and the people at the hospital said I should go back to work. I didn't feel equipped to go back because I had been away from it since '38. I didn't feel I was able to do what was required of me, so finally I went to a couple refresher meetings. It was just talk, and you didn't really learn anything. That was after the new hospital was built [1951]. Eventually, I signed in to work part time when they needed me. I waited about ten days before they called me. I went to work, and that was the worst day of my life! The nurse wanted me to do the medications, give all the shots, and at that time there was a lot of them. She gave me the cards to go by, and I didn't even recognize the drugs. When I was last working there was no such thing as penicillin or any of the drugs that they were using, so every time I opened a bottle, I had to study the literature on them, and it was awful. Then, when I got all the shots given, I had to do all the oral medications, and there was just as many of those. You had to do this several times a day before three o'clock in the afternoon. By the time three o'clock came, I thought my head was up seventy stories high, and I felt as though I was going to pass out. It was so hard, and they didn't give us any indoctrination at all. You just went to work. They don't do that at all anymore. Anytime you get hired you get a refresher course in whatever you're going to do. But that was wicked, and, as it turned out, after about two weeks I was working eight shifts in a week. They kept calling me all the time, and I said I can't do this; you're going to have to schedule me at regular times. And they did, and I worked five days a week for a long time.

Laina continued her nursing career for more than thirty years. Ted died when their twins were only twelve years old. Laina's final years were spent at the Country Club Retirement Campus in Ashtabula. She died on December 5, 2002, at the age of ninety-one.

Viena Salo Hejduk

My father's name was Frank Isak Salo. He was born in Panelia, Finland. When he was a young man he went to Tornio, up north, near the Swedish border, to work on a railroad being built there. He met my mother there, and her name was Ellen Aliina Trukki. When my dad left Finland in 1904, he had an understanding that my mother would follow him to America, sometime later, and then they would be married.

So my mother went by herself to America in 1906, headed for Erie, Pennsylvania, where my father was a dockworker on Lake Erie. My mother had a funny experience when she came here. She was on the train coming to Erie and decided to buy a banana from the boy who went around selling them in a basket, along with other things. She looked at the banana, then looked around to see if anyone around her had bought one. They hadn't, so she didn't know what to do with it. She didn't know if she should eat the outside, or the whole thing, or what. So she finally threw it out the window!

When she got off the train, there was no one to meet her, and she didn't know what to do again. Evidently my father had no idea when she was to arrive. Then she saw her trunk being put on a wagon, and she went and sat on it. She then went where the trunk went.

My father and mother were married on October 7, 1906. My mother wore a lovely orchid-colored gown that I used to play "dress-up" in when I was a little girl. In 1908 my sister Martha was born, but she died of pneumonia before her first birthday. My parents had a picture of her in an oval frame that they always kept hanging in their bedroom. That way, the rest of us kids always knew who Martha was.

I was born next, on May 13, 1910, in Erie. Then came my sister, Aino Marja (Mary), and my brother, Earl Isaac. There was another boy, but he lived only one day. I was only four then, but I can remember seeing the baby in a white suit, laying in a small casket. We rode to the cemetery with a horse and buggy.

My dad worked on the docks seven days a week, and ten-hour days. He got one dollar a day. Then he heard railroads in Ashtabula were hiring, so we moved there by train, even taking our furniture. This was in the summer of 1915. We rented a house on Bell Court, then later bought a house on Auburn Street [a section of West Thirty-eighth Street] in the area they used to call Forty Acres.

My mother made Finnish foods every day. She made her own bread, and she made *nisua* every week. The three of us used to walk uptown with my mother to shop. Before going home, we would stop in a grocery store and buy corned-beef slices and a special rye bread. We could hardly wait to get home for the treat!

I went to grade school at the west end of town, then to Park Junior High. On the first day when I was a freshman at Ashtabula High, the teacher called out my name with the boys' roster, and I was so embarrassed. My name was spelled "Vieno" then, so I changed the *o* to an *a* and that's how it was spelled ever after. Back in Finland, my father's last name was Logerbom, but he changed it to Salo, and I'm very glad. I wouldn't have wanted to grow up with the last name of Logerbom! I grew up speaking both Finnish and English.

Although my parents both became American citizens, my mother never learned much English. My father spoke some, but it wasn't very good.

I wore long woolen stockings in the winter, and we used to ride our sleds down a hill by the lake shore. If we didn't have a sled we'd use a piece of cardboard instead.

We used to go to the steam bath on West Thirtieth Street. I loved the steam bath. I would sit on the top bench, and we would smack ourselves all over with birch twigs. I wish I could still go into the sauna, but I can't because of high blood pressure. My mother's sister, Hilda, was the only other relative who came to America. She married Victor Mellin and they bought the sauna on West Thirtieth.

I remember our family going to Sovinto Hall for dances, plays, and to celebrate Finland's Independence Day [December 6, 1917]. We were members of Bethany Lutheran Church, so we went to church picnics in the summers. We would drive out to the country, too, for picnics. We had a 1924 Plymouth, and it would take us a half-day to get to Dorset.

Before we had a car, and, since we didn't live in the Harbor, the "uptown Finns" rented Messiah Lutheran Church on Hiawatha Avenue for Sunday afternoons so the kids could have a Sunday school. I even taught Sunday school when I was fifteen. The kids were five-year-olds, and I remember some of them were Arnold Erickson, Alfred Hanel, and John Kahelin. I was just fifteen when I got my first job, too. I was a maid for the Sanborn family who lived on Sanborn Road.

I was confirmed at Bethany Lutheran when I was sixteen. Confirmation classes were held during the summer, and we had to study a catechism written in Finnish. After I graduated from Ashtabula High School in 1928, I attended Spencerian Business College in Cleveland. I roomed with a doctor's family in Cleveland Heights. I did housework for them before and after school hours. I got my room and board, plus $1.50 a week that was used for my streetcar fare to the school. My first secretarial job was in the office of a paint factory. During the Depression, I sent money home to my parents to help pay for their utilities. I once got a twenty-five dollar Christmas bonus, and I sent that back home, too. They were able to buy a new linoleum and a heater for their bathroom with that money.

When Mary finished school, we both worked in Cleveland. We stayed with a Juhola family in Lakewood. Mary worked in a beauty shop that was next door to a grocery store, and that's where Jim Hejduk worked. Jim would sometimes give Mary a ride home. One time he stopped by to see Mary, and

I answered the door and told him Mary wasn't home. He said that was okay, because he was thinking about seeing me.

Jim and I were married on October 7, 1934. My husband was of Bohemian descent, but my parents didn't mind that he wasn't Finnish. I kept on working as a stenographer at a steel company, and in 1937 we bought a house in Parma. In 1939, we bought a 103-acre farm in Brunswick so we could be closer to Jim's mother and a disabled brother who needed our help. We had an old farmhouse there that needed a lot of work, but we didn't farm the land because Jim was a manager at a Kroger store then.

I worked for Johnson, Locke & Steel Company throughout the war years, and by the time I quit in the summer of 1945 I was secretary to the vice-president of sales. I was expecting my first child then, and Mary Ellen was born in December of 1945. Then we had James Alan in 1947 and Alice Elizabeth in 1949. We remodeled the farmhouse, too.

My husband died in 1959, and my mother died in 1960. I visited family here in Ashtabula quite often over the years, but I didn't move back until 1979. Then I went back to Bethany Lutheran Church and belonged to the Women of Bethany. I later joined the Finnish-American Heritage Association. I go along with Bethany's "Friendly Visitors" to area nursing homes, and I help out baking *nisua* for the church's bake sales. [*Nisua* sales are still being held as a fund-raiser for Bethany Lutheran. It has been said that Bethany was "built with *nisua*."]

At the time of Viena's 1996 interview, she was still living independently at age eighty-six. She later moved to the Country Club Retirement Campus in Ashtabula. She died on November 12, 2005, at the age of ninety-five, and is buried in Townline Cemetery, Brunswick, Ohio.

Sylvia J. Holso Waltari

My mother, Hanna Ilmi Krook, came to Ashtabula first, from Karstula. My father, Jacob Holso, emigrated from Karstula, Finland. Each of them had relatives here when they came, I think in the early 1900s. They were married in 1907 in the first Bethany Lutheran Church by Pastor Frans Kava. [Kava pastored Bethany from 1907 to 1912, when the church had the lengthy name of "The Harbor Finnish Evangelical Lutheran Bethany Congregation."]

My sister Lillian was born in 1908, and I was born August 30, 1911. We first rented a place on Joseph Avenue. Later, we moved to the second floor of

Hukari's store. My parents never owned their own home. My father worked on the New York Central Railroad, and he was also a blacksmith's helper. My mother did a lot of house cleaning for people, and she even cleaned at the Talvola Bakery. She also worked in the woolen mills that were on Bridge Street. She did laundry, too, for one of the doctor's families; she did it for many years. She had a wagon that she pulled the laundry with. Then, one day, the doctor's wife was missing a napkin, or something small like that, and she accused my mother of taking it. So my mother was so upset that she said that's the end of that job!

I remember Torppa Hall on Joseph Avenue. Some people came from New York to show their plays. When they had dances, Helmi Luoma and I—when we were young—would go to the door and listen to the music and peek in. The Koykkas were the smoothest dancers. They had a balcony in that hall, and that's where they chased all the kids, so we'd see all those plays. My friend, Helmi, was only sixteen when she graduated from high school. We've known each other for so long. I remember all the games we played as kids, and we would go around the whole Harbor at night; nowadays I would be afraid to go out at night. I wouldn't even walk to the church.

One of our neighbors used to ask me, "Have you started confirmation school yet?" So I went to confirmation school at the "little church" [Finnish Congregational] because it was only for two weeks. At Bethany, I would have had to go the whole year.

Elvi [Herlevi] and I went to summer school at the Yellow Hall—the brick one—and that's where I learned to read Finnish. I went to see lot of concerts at Sovinto because we lived right near there.

We always went to the beach, too. One early April, Elvi and I went down there when ice was still on the lake. We were down there wading and, when I happened to look up the hill, there was my mother looking down at us. Boy, did I get the worst licking in my life. But maybe I'm paying for it now, because when I was in high school I had rheumatic fever that weakened my heart.

Lillian and I went to the Washington and Jackson schools, and I graduated from Harbor High School in 1929. During the Depression my father worked off and on for the railroad, but he was too proud to ask for assistance of any kind. So my mother went for food stamps, and it was during the Depression years when she worked most outside the home.

I went to work as a clerk-secretary at the Ashtabula Corrugated Box Company [later, Inland Container]. I met Loren Waltari there when he worked there, too, and years later Loren retired from there. We were married on

November 2, 1940, and our daughter, Kay, was born in 1945. We first rented an apartment, then we bought a house on Myrtle Avenue, around 1953, when Kay was eight years old. My aunt, Helmi Olson, didn't have a television set, so she visited us every Saturday night so she could watch "The Lawrence Welk Show."

My sister Lillian clerked at Turner's Drug Store for fifty years, and she bought her own house on Lake Road West. Loren and Lillian both died in 1976, but I stayed in my home on Myrtle Avenue and kept busy with activities at Bethany Lutheran Church.

In 1997 Sylvia moved in with her daughter, Kay Trawick, in Centerville, Massachusetts, on Cape Cod. Kay's children, Karen and Sam, also lived nearby. Sylvia died there on May 18, 2003, at the age of ninety-two.

Ilona Korpela Kotila

My grandfather, John Aho, left Kauhava, Finland, the first time, in the late 1800s and went to Ishpeming, Michigan. Our family name has been changed, but I have a different reason. In Finland, in the 1800s, if a wife-to-be was from a rich farm family, the husband had to take her name. My grandmother's name was Alexandra (Sandra) Korpela, and she was from Alajärvi. Her parents chose the groom for her, and he was thirty-eight, and my grandmother was eighteen. Then his name became John Korpela. My mother was born when my grandmother was nineteen, and my grandmother died during childbirth. They named the baby Sandra, too, and my grandfather never remarried. My mother was brought up by the maid, or the hired help, and there was just this one maid there all her life.

My mother and father [also named John] met in Alajärvi and were married there in 1898. My four brothers were born first, in Finland. Then my father left Finland to go to Ontario, Canada, and he took my oldest brother, Charles, with him. My father started the Korpela Lumber Company, near Sudbury. My mother stayed with her father on the farm, then in 1911 my father wanted my mother to come to Canada with him but she didn't want to leave her father when he was aging already. So my father threatened to take the boys from her, and she finally gave in. At that time, the youngest brother was two years of age; as soon as they got to Canada, he got pneumonia and died. My mother was pregnant with my brother Frank on the way from Finland, and so he was born in July. They named him exactly the same name of the boy that just died. My mother had eleven children altogether, but four of them died before they were adults.

My oldest brother was nineteen when I was born, and the next brother was fourteen. There had been a sister and three brothers who died between them. I was the bottom of the list, the youngest, after my two sisters, Aili (Lehto) and Sylvia (Perttula). I was born on October 18, 1915, in Nemegos, Ontario, and my father died three weeks before I was born. Mother was left with seven children. She kept boarders, mostly lumbermen, and that's the way she supported seven children.

She was a marvelous cook. That's why we had so many boarders around, because she made such good food. She always made them feel at home, and she always told us children not to ever insult them, because that was her livelihood. She'd go in the barn before six o'clock and milk eight cows before she fed the boarders. She told me that she didn't have much time for me because there was nights when she only slept two hours, and that's the only time I was with her when I was a baby. She had my brother, Ted, look after me and my sister, Sylvia, who was only one year older than me. When Ted was ten years old he was always stuck with two babies on each side. Sometimes he pinched us to make us cry real hard so he had an excuse to go out and play. That was some childhood!

I went to school in Nemegos, but there was no local church at that time. We had the traditional Christmas tree, but in those days not much presents. There was a Finnish hall, where they had dances and plays, and I had a lot of companionship in the neighborhood. They were French, and we taught them Finnish and they taught us French. We spoke French before we spoke English, even before we went to school. So I still remember it even though I was here for forty years and didn't hear any French. When I went back to Canada, thirty years ago, I was surprised that my brain retained it. It all came back—just like swimming. So I speak three languages. Now, when the younger people go to school there, it's a have to.

I went to Sudbury to work when I was very young—in 1930 and 1931—when the Communist movement was fierce. They used to have parades on Elm Street, and in 1931 the head of the Communist society was there on May Day. They were marching to the city hall and the fire department came and put their hoses on them. The Communist movement was so strong that they almost forced the young people to join their society. I objected to that, and that's why I left there.

I went first to New York City. I did domestic work and took care of children. Those were the Depression years, and then I heard I might find better work in Cleveland. So I took the train to Cleveland, Ohio, and worked in a ladies' wear store. I didn't meet my husband, John Kotila, right away, but I met him through his mother, Sofie Kotila, and she lived in Ashtabula. Sofie (Lundstrom) had come to Ashtabula from Raahe, Finland, with her father, a Swede, in 1891, when she was only fourteen years old. The Kotilas came from Pattijärvi. Sofie married Andrew Kotila in 1898, and John was the first child of eight children. Then there was Oscar, Herman, Ray, Victor, Gertrude, Freda, and Arthur.

I married John Kotila in 1935 and came to live in Ashtabula. He had been a widower for six years and had two children, Earl and June. Then together we had Sonja who was born in 1936.

My husband was a building contractor, and he worked as a boat-building foreman during the war. When we were first married we lived on Thayer Avenue for six years. Then we bought some property on Ninevah Road and Lake Road West corners with five acres and an old house. After the war, John started building in a housing area, and we sold the houses. He continued contracting and built a lot of houses. He was a very good architect, though he hadn't gone to school. He did a very good job of remodeling and was very capable of drawing. His biggest desire, if he would have had the education, would have been as a bridge builder or engineer. When we crossed the Mackinac Bridge the first time, he almost cried, because he said that was his dream, that this is what he would have liked to have done if he would have had a chance for an education. He was very good at drawing and his writing was excellent. He was considered a well-rounded guy and knew how to get things done. It was amazing what he could do without real high or formal education.

When we lived on Lake Road, Sonja went to Ashtabula High School. She came home one day, when she was fifteen, and said she had joined the society of Future Teachers of America. She always carried through with what she said she was going to do, so she went to college and taught school until she retired. She met Gerald Corlew in 1956, and they were married in 1958. He became superintendent of maintenance for Buckeye Local Schools in 1960. They have two children: Rebecca, who is also a teacher, and Jay, who teaches and is a football coach.

After my husband died, and my stepchildren and Sonja had married, I felt I would go back to Canada because my sisters were there. So in 1968 I went to Sudbury, where the International Nickel Company is located. There are lots of other industries, and two large universities. It's in an area of beautiful lakes, and it's hilly and rocky. It's a large city, and they have an historical area and, also, a science center that tells all about how Sudbury was created by a meteorite falling, and that's how they found the nickel. There's a lot of Finns there who first came when the railroad was built around 1887. The Finnish rest home system was created there fifteen years ago when the Finland-born and second generation were getting old. Now it's a sixteen-million-dollar senior center. The Finlandia has ninety apartments, a big social room, a chapel, and saunas. Four different ministers visit once a month, and they have all kinds of social doings. My nephew gave twenty-eight acres for this center out of his 150 acres that he owned within the city. He made it through World War II as a bomber pilot, but four of his crew died. He was missing for eight months, but when he came back he wanted to do something for his city. He made a real success of the lumber company when he took it over from my brother, Charlie, in 1969. He's now seventy-seven, and he sold the lumber mill industry three years ago for a big profit.

I come here [Ashtabula] to visit once a year, but I have it so much better there. I wouldn't dare to come back on account of the socialized medicine. We have very good doctors and three large hospitals. They even have a special heart hospital for open-heart surgery.

I still have the big five-liter, copper coffeepot that my father brought from Finland the first time he came. My brother owned my mother's little house where she lived in the last years of her life, and he would go back there to go hunting. So I asked him one time when he went if he'd bring me the coffeepot. So he brought me the pot covered with black soot, then laughed at me, and asked what I was going to do with that crummy thing. And I just said, "Who laughs last, laughs best." My mother had used it as an oil can, but I didn't care. It was a treasure to me because it signified to the whole family how hard she worked, and how she supported us. It was that copper pot that had been our coffeepot on our stove, and from childhood on we remembered the boarders pouring their coffee. So I brought it to the United States and had it chemically cleaned and lacquered several coats. Now all I have to do is dust it. I value the most all the dents in it.

The nephew who owned the lumber company that he inherited from his father said he would give a million dollars for it if he could get it. One time, when I was living in the senior center, he brought a bunch of those big shots into my small apartment, and I thought, "What on earth does he have up his sleeve now?" He lifted that coffeepot from my hutch and lifted it to the ceiling. He said, "I'm from my grandmother who really had *sisu*; she supported seven children with this coffeepot and never took a penny of welfare because she was always so proud."

Ilona died in Sudbury on December 26, 2000, when she was eighty-five.

Reino Johannes Saarikoski (Ray Koski)

My father was Simon Saarikoski, and he was born in Nurmo, Finland, in 1884. My mother, Sofia (Gustafson), was born in Nurmo in 1887. They were married in 1905, and my father left Finland in 1907 while my mother waited until he could send for her. My father had friends in Waukegan, Illinois, and that's the first place he headed for.

He stayed in a boarding house, and it wasn't too long before he got a job, or many jobs, one right after another. One job was peddling milk. There was a bad dog on his route that always gave him a hard time, so one day when the dog came at him, he grabbed a milk bottle and let the dog have it. I guess it didn't do any harm to the dog, but it left him alone after that and stayed pretty well away from him.

Another job he had was at the Karo syrup factory. He said the whole roof was wooden beams and planks, and they had open kettles down below where they cooked the syrup. When the weather was warm, why—insects—and whatever they had on the roof, kept dropping down into the syrup. He never cared for Karo after that, but I suppose they had some kind of system where they screened the syrup.

My dad worked two or three jobs there, and another one was in a steel mill, working with steel wire. Finally he had enough money saved so he could send money back for the wife to come to Waukegan in 1909. I guess I was the love child when she came over, as I was the child she bore on March 20, 1910. I was followed by my sister, Elma; then a brother, Paavo; another sister, Elsie; then two more brothers, Arvo and Lauri. Elsie contracted infantile paralysis when she was only ten months old. She was left partially crippled on her right side; yet she went to school and graduated, but never married.

My dad heard about a railroad job in Conneaut, Ohio, so he packed up whatever we had at the time, which wasn't too much, and we headed for Conneaut. We lived on Day Street, and the thing that stays in my mind is the shanty in the backyard where all the men from the docks came to wash their hands. I could smell the tar soap they all used, and that smell stayed with me for a long time.

My dad was then offered a railroad job in Ashtabula. First, though, there were friends of his, an older couple, who wanted to move on a farm, but they thought they couldn't take care of it themselves. So my dad thought he could hold down his regular job and bicycle back and forth to West Springfield to help them farm. But even for a young man to take care of a farm, his own job, and bicycle back and forth, was more than he anticipated. When he heard the same railroad company would hire him in Ashtabula, he decided to move there.

He had a neighbor, John Lahti, who had a horse, and my dad had another horse. They had a good-sized hay wagon where they loaded all our belongings, then covered them with some carpeting because a light snow was falling. They headed for Ashtabula, but along the way there was a toll bridge they had to cross, and the charge for a load that size was seventy-five cents. Well, my dad thought he couldn't afford to spend the money, so they went down the hill under the bridge. But the hill was so icy they had a heck of a time getting up the other side, and one of the horses threw a shoe. But finally they got the load up the hill. Then they lost one hour getting the horse shod at a blacksmith's. It was about a fourteen-mile trip; they started around 10 A.M. and arrived in Ashtabula after dark.

They had a place lined up—the Kaura house on Bridge Street—but they left everything on the wagon and put it in the livery stable for overnight. The next day was Christmas Day and that's when they moved everything into the house. That was 1914, when I was four years old. We weren't in that house very long before we moved to the next street up the hill—Market Street—which is West Sixth Street now. We lived next to a sauna. It was an old-fashioned kind of steam bath that produced steam in a boiler, and when you wanted steam you opened a valve and steam came into the room. It had a ladies' room side and the men's side each with a wash and steam room.

About that time Dad heard that Franz Holmstrom was building himself a new house in the "squirrel woods" area and was going to sell the house on Oak Street, or West Eighth. So Dad bought the house on West Eighth Street and we moved there. Signe and Harry Olson lived on one side of us, and the Jacobson family was on the other side. Jacobson was the conductor of the Humina Band at that time. There was a Lahti boy living nearby who was invited to go to Russia, where they said it was to be a new heaven and a new earth. So he went to Russia and was never heard from again.

In that area were all the small stores and apartment and boarding houses. Down the hill was where all the kids would bring their sleds because there was no traffic there. And old man Maenpaa lived on top of that hill. He was a typical type of Finn who would come up to Sovinto Hall, where he was very active, and he walked two or three steps ahead of his wife, leaving her back there "in her place." A lot of the men gathered at Kukka Matti's place to sit around and talk, just like we have a gang of men called the "Finnish Mafia" who meet at the bakery and coffeeshop nowadays. Farther down was a confectionery and the Salvation Army Building, where all the sailors spent nights. They had nice facilities. At the top of what we called "office hill" was a business office for all the navigation of the ships, and down below it were the ore docks and the ore operations. They're not there anymore as the docks have moved up on the point farther out.

Rasmus Confectionery was across from Sovinto Hall. Rasmus used to have a saloon, but his girlfriend said she wouldn't have anything to do with him as long as he had the saloon. When he had the saloon, and had any trouble there with the drunks, he'd take them by the scruff of the neck and dump them outside, saying: "Voi, voi . . ." [mild expletive]. Finally he dumped the saloon and married the girlfriend. There were about fifteen saloons on those streets at one time.

But there were churches, too, and they were known by whoever was pastor there at the time. Mannerkorpi's church was the old Bethany Lutheran; Mannerkorpi was there from 1912 to 1917. Lehtinen was at the "little church," or Finnish Congregational. I remember going to Lehtinen's church. He took his preaching so seriously that he'd get tears in his eyes when he began to preach. He was a very emotional man. And there was the first Zion Lutheran on the opposite corner from Bethany.

We kids used to look through the downstairs windows of the Electric Laundry and watch women running the big sheets through the rollers. I remember when the Electric Laundry burned later, when we lived about three miles out. I saw massive smoke and jumped into the car and watched it burn. It was all wood, and the chemicals in there kept the fire going.

I went to Harbor High School, and did the art work for Harbor's 1927 yearbook, the year I graduated. I then went to the Arts and Crafts Institute in Detroit. After three and a half years there, I was qualified to work as a commercial artist in the 1930s. I also taught art and drafting at Harbor High for a while. I legally changed my name to Reino John Koski, but I'm better known as Ray.

On June 14, 1941, I married Maxine Smith. She's of Swedish descent. Then I was drafted into the army, in July 1942, and served in the U.S. Army Signal Corps. I was in the radar section in Puerto Rico where I tracked planes. One day I was tracking a plane when it disappeared abruptly from the screen. I later learned that a good friend of mine, Ray Alpine, was on board that plane and killed when it crashed into the side of a mountain. In fact, Ray had been a member of my wedding party.

I transferred later to the public relations' section of the headquarters in San Juan. I always carried my watercolors with me, and I was once asked to do a portrait of General William Shield for *Time* magazine. After that I got involved during much of the war with painting and sketching scenes in all the U.S. posts in the Caribbean and northern South America.

After the war I returned to Ashtabula and got a job with Matt Kujala, who was an architect and builder. I did design and drafting work while I was taking more courses at Fenn College [now Cleveland State]. I passed the Ohio State architect's exam and became licensed on July 10, 1956. We became Kujala and Koski, designing and building such projects as the new Bethany Lutheran Church and its parsonage, Good Shepherd Lutheran Church in Conneaut, the Walnut Beach bathhouse, the Ashtabula County Courthouse in Jefferson, and the Harbor-Topky Library. I also designed and built most of my own house where I live with Maxine and our son, David. Our house is of contemporary design and was built in 1951 at the end of Arcola Drive on the lakefront.

Maxine worked for the law firm of Warren and Young beginning in 1937, taking only six months off when David was born in 1952. Throughout the years we traveled extensively all over the United States, including Alaska; different European countries, including Finland; Hawaii; Panama; and across lower Canada by train.

I retired from the architectural firm in 1985, and Maxine retired from the Warren and Young offices in 1987.

Ray was a member of Bethany Lutheran Church, where he served on various committees, the church council, and he sang in the chancel choir. In 1941, he designed the front cover for Bethany's fiftieth anniversary booklet and created the anniversary logo for Bethany's 100th year celebrations in 1991. He designed the logo for the Finnish-American Heritage Association in 1995, and his talents were also used in designing the cover of Harbor High's 100th anniversary booklet. Ray also continued his involvement with the Ashtabula Arts Center where he worked with ceramics and paintings. In 1997 he was presented with the Harbor

Coalition Certificate of Appreciation that honored him for his many years of dedication to his country, his church, and his community. Ray Koski died in his home on July 9, 2000, at the age of ninety.

Ellen Luoma Fitting

My father's name was Oscar Luoma. He left Ylihärmä by himself in 1907. My mother was left behind with my two sisters, Senia and Mary, until my dad earned enough money to send them tickets. My dad worked first in the cranberry bogs of Massachusetts, then he worked in the Pennsylvania coal mines. Then he traveled to Ashtabula Harbor because he somehow heard there was work there at the docks and that other Finns were living there.

My mother, Maria, and her two little girls, left Finland a few years later. Her father went with them as far as where the boat [to England] was docked. Then he just disappeared and didn't even say goodbye.

When they went through Ellis Island, of course my mother couldn't speak English, so they hung a directional sign on her, and she and the girls were pushed along. There was no one to meet them at the train station in Ashtabula, but a Mr. Tikkanen took them to the Harbor, where my dad was then living on Cherry Street [West Ninth Street].

Later, my father built a house on Atlantic Street [West Thirteenth Street]. By then my sister, Martha, was born, and my brother, John. They had had another son in Finland, but he died in infancy. I was the youngest, born on January 9, 1913.

I started school in the Washington building, then went to Thayer School, which was at the corner of Carpenter and Stowe roads, until the eighth grade. I missed a year of high school, because my parents wouldn't allow me to have a mandatory vaccination. I finally saw Dr. Collander, who gave me a "scratch," and then I returned to school. In high school I participated in track meets. I was a champion runner, broad jumper, high jumper, and shot putter. I also played basketball at Sovinto Hall. I graduated from Harbor High School in 1932.

We had a barn with several cows, so my mother delivered milk to families on Huron Street [West Tenth]. Then, when we moved to Tryon Road, we had a dairy herd of thirty cows. My dad ran the "Luoma Dairy." He bottled the milk and delivered it to homes. He was also a carpenter—a master carpenter, they used to say. So he learned enough English to talk to people when he delivered milk or worked as a carpenter, but my mother never learned but a few words of English during her entire life.

My mother always prepared Finnish foods. We had rice pudding with fruit sauce, potato soup, rye bread, *nisua,* and our favorite dessert was *vispii puuro* [whipped pudding, usually flavored with grape juice].

The whole family used to go to Torpa Hall, especially to watch plays when Senia was acting in them. We went to dances there, too, but my parents never danced. Finns used to congregate at a summer place, *synninlaaksa,* in Finnish. People would camp there, and there was a sauna there, and we'd grill meat and cook coffee. Our family went there a lot. It became Stone's Long Beach, out on Lake Road West, but the beach there has all eroded. We used to go to movies a lot, too, at the Harbor Theatre.

My first job was picking strawberries at two cents a quart when I was eight. But I saved all my money, and bought my first pair of patent-leather shoes for ten dollars. During my high-school years, in the summers, I worked as a cook's helper in Maple Manor at Geneva-on-the-Lake.

Floyd Fitting was working at the Cleveland Electric Illuminating Company in Ashtabula when I met him. We were married in August of 1937, and our first home was on Route 20 in Saybrook Township. Our daughter, Joanne, was born in 1938; and Fred, our son, was born in 1939. I worked as a meter reader for the water company, too, and then we bought ten acres of lakefront property, along with another couple. There was just a bicycle track on those acres, and we rented bicycles by the hour. Later, when the other couple decided to get out of the business, they leased us their five acres.

About that time, Floyd decided to build a miniature golf course, and he had other plans for it, but he died in 1948 with complications after pneumonia. So I was a widow at thirty-five and had two children to support. I kept the lake property and continued to rent out campsites. In those days, most campers had tents or real small trailers. And I worked other places, too. I worked for the *Star Beacon,* for Ashtabula Rubber, for Nystrom Cleaners, and I delivered dry cleaning for Martell Cleaners. The kids and I lived with my folks on the dairy farm. Then when the kids were in their early teens, they were able to help at the campgrounds. I had a road put in to the beach, and people camped down there, too. We also had a boathouse built, and we rented out fishing boats. When we started to get more and more campers, my dad built a concrete-block restroom building, and that's still there. But in the mid-seventies we had such a big storm that the beach road was wiped out, and so was the boathouse, and lots of trees, so that put an end to beach camping. Over the years, we've tried different things to stop beach erosion. We finally constructed an armored-rock wall, and that seems to be holding up. So I kept busy mowing grass, trimming, and cleaning up debris from the beach. And the restrooms always had to be cleaned. I believe it was the park that kept me young.

I remarried in 1963 and helped my husband with his restaurant business, but still kept up with the campgrounds' work. Before ten years were up, we were divorced, and I was back full time at the park.

It wasn't until she was eighty-six that Ellen relinquished the arduous chores of the campgrounds to Joanne and Fred. She now shares a home with Joanne, built in front of the park, where she can still keep an eye on the campgrounds and on Lake Erie with its seasonal changes. At ninety-two (2005), Ellen has outlived her siblings, yet she enjoys visits from her ten grandchildren, ten great-grandchildren, and three great-great-grandchildren.

Mamie Wiirtanen Maki

My father, Urho Wiirtanen, was born on September 16, 1886, in Maaria, Finland. My mother, Liisi Kangas, was born on May 21, 1893, in Piippola, Finland. I think my mother came to this country first. I remember she told me that she had to go in third class. She could hear babies crying, and the smell wasn't all that great. My mother went to Bisbee, Arizona, first, but I don't know why. I have these postcards, though, that were sent to my mother in Bisbee from Finland. They have dates of 1910 and 1913, and they're Christmas and New Year's greetings, printed in Finnish. My mother and father met and married in Arizona, but I never was told anything about that. My sister, Irja, was born in Arizona on November 7, 1916, then they all went back to Finland after that.

I was born in Turku on August 13, 1919, then, when I was only eleven months old, we all went back to the United States. We went first to Detroit, Michigan, because my folks had friends there. Before too long, we moved to the west side of Cleveland, Ohio. My dad worked as a carpenter, and they bought this large house on Church Avenue in Cleveland. There was a rooming house, and then there was a separate house, so it was like a package deal. They rented out light housekeeping rooms and sleeping rooms. We lived on the first floor of the smaller house and rented out more rooms on the second floor.

When my folks went to register me at Kentucky School, the lady in the principal's office asked my father about my birth certificate. He could speak English a little better than my mother, so he told the lady that my birth certificate was burned in the church in Finland. Then he told my mother, in Finnish, what the lady wanted. My mother said, in Finnish, "There's the child right there. What more proof do they need?" That was my first encounter in school. By the time I went to school, my father shortened our name to Wirta, and my mother always went by Lizzie.

In summertime we went on picnics. It seemed like we always knew families who lived on a farm. My mother would always take food even though it was hard times. My mother was a good cook, so it's hard to say what I really liked best. I liked the sour-milk pancakes that she usually made on Saturday. She wasn't a cake maker, but her *nisua* was just wonderful. If we had any kind of celebrations with another family, my mother was always the *nisua* bringer. We had a two-burner gas stove in the basement, and that's where we heated water to do all our laundry, and the towels and sheets for the rooming house.

My folks liked to go to dances in the Finn halls in Cleveland. One hall had doings every Saturday, and then audience chairs were pushed aside and the hall would be for dancing. As a little child, me and my sister always had to take a nap on Saturday so we could go to the dances with our folks. We didn't have a grandma or grandpa or any babysitters, so we always had to take that nap so we could go with them.

We didn't have any toys, but sometimes our dad would bring home little scraps of wood, or little tiles left over from a bathroom, and we'd build things to play with. The other carpenters could take scraps home, too, but Dad thought we got our share.

My father was off work during the Depression, but we did have the rooming house. Rent was only two or three dollars a week, though, and some people couldn't even pay that. Quite a few owed my folks money, but when good times came they never came and paid it back. They didn't even try to come and pay them. I never got over that. I don't care what kind of story they tell me, I'm never going to rent to people.

I remember the winters were cold in Cleveland, like they are in Ashtabula. I had a nice spring coat with a tam, but my mother thought we should buy a heavier coat for me. And I said, "Ma, I have this coat right here. I can put my sweater underneath it and it'll be all right." I had a long distance to walk to all my schools, and my mother felt so bad that I didn't get no coat. I was a real healthy kid, and I didn't feel bad. I knew it was real poor times.

I wouldn't call it a job, but when I was maybe fifteen years old, I went to sweep out a Finnish man's shoemaker shop, and I got a dime for it. After I graduated from high school, in 1938, my first real job was as a waitress on Detroit Avenue in Cleveland. And that's where I met Tauno Maki. We were married on July 21, 1944. We were married in Cleveland by a justice of peace. Only my mother, my sister, and a couple friends were with us.

Tauno was six years in the U.S. Navy on a submarine. During the war, I worked for Standard Tool and for White Sewing Machine Company in the "Flats" [along the Cuyahoga River]. Those places were converted to make tools for the war effort.

We first lived in Cleveland, but we lived on a naval base in California when our son, Lauri, was born on July 13, 1946. Then Lauri and I moved in with Tauno's mother in Ashtabula until Tauno got out of the navy. Tauno was born in Ashtabula on March 24, 1915. His folks' names were Mary and Herman Maki.

When Tauno got out of the navy, we rented our own place. It was a cold-water flat on West Ninth Street. I'm embarrassed to tell these things. We had a hot water tank before, and when we came here, we went down a little bit.

In 1947 we bought the fish market with Ray and Mae Hill, but the Hills stayed in the partnership just a few months. Our daughter, Kristine, was born on June 25, 1952.

The fish market did so well that we were able to open Hil-Mak Sea Food Restaurant on April 12, 1972. Kristine worked in both the market and restaurant with us for thirty years.

In 1978 Tauno and I took a trip to Finland. We went to Turku, where I was born, and I saw my grandparents' house. My cousin, Heikki, sent me a picture of the house when we first started the restaurant, and I had it framed later.

We lived in an apartment over the restaurant, but when Tauno died, in 1993, I lived with my daughter in her house for a few years. Then I moved back into the apartment in 2004.

Mamie's son Lauri is now president of Hil-Mak Sea Food Restaurant and his wife Karen is manager. They have one son, David, who has pursued other interests. At eighty-six (2005), Mamie goes downstairs and begins "prep work" each morning for the restaurant but takes Sundays and Mondays off.

Building the break wall in Ashtabula Harbor to prevent sand building up at the entrance to the harbor, ca. 1907. (Photo courtesy of Petros Collection)

Bakery wagons lined up in front of Bjerstedt's Bakery, where some Finnish men and women were employed. West Fourth Street, Ashtabula Harbor. (Photo courtesy of Petros Collection)

Facing page: George Wahlstrom (left) and unidentified man in 1927 at the train station in New York before setting sail for their Finland concert tour. A concert was given in New York prior to sailing. (Photo courtesy of Myra Wahlstrom and FACC)

This photo of Conneaut's Kilpi Temperance Hall, as it was first named, is believed to have been taken in 1899 at the hall's dedication. This hall still remains on Buffalo Street, and is now the home of the Conneaut Community Center for the Arts. The building was entered in the National Register of Historic Places in 1977. The observation platform on the very top was removed sometime over the years, but it must have provided a grand view of Lake Erie. (Photo courtesy of Penny Armeni, executive director, Conneaut Community Center for the Arts)

Senia (Fraback) and Robert Willehad Nieminen in their April 1916 wedding portrait. "Bill" Nieminen emigrated alone from Finland in 1914 and worked as a farmhand on the Fraback farm. Senia was the oldest of fourteen children. (Photo courtesy of Rebecca Niemi Sloan)

Lempi Kajander emigrated from Finland in 1920 with her parents, who then returned to Finland the following year. Lempi remained in America and most likely had this photo taken for her parents before they left. Lempi lived to the age of 103. (Photo courtesy of Eleanor Stevenson)

Otto and Marja Kajander, ca. 1928. Photo taken in Voikka, Finland, for their fiftieth wedding anniversary and sent to their daughter, Lempi, in Ashtabula. (Photo courtesy of Eleanor Stevenson)

The swing bridge straddled the Ashtabula River, connecting Bridge Street with East Sixth Street. This bridge replaced the pontoon bridge in 1889 and was in use until 1925. (Photo courtesy of Petros Collection)

Later Arrivals, 1910–1955

Emigration from Finland dwindled during the World War I years because Germany was suspected to have mined the North and Baltic seas, making sailing hazardous.

A small percentage of Finnish men returned to their homeland during winters when the lower Great Lakes froze and shipping halted. Some went home and bought land with their earnings and remained, while others returned to America. Winter employment for other dock laborers included cutting ice in the river for commercial use, going farther south to work in coal mines, or heading north to work in the logging industry.

Immigration to the United States slowed even more when the quota system was enacted in 1924. During the Great Depression, when more people left the United States than those entering, some Finns were among them.

During the World War II years, Finns here were generous in sending "Finnish relief" packages of food, clothing, and money to relatives and friends who were enduring hardships during these war-torn years. And many emigrants, who left Finland to escape conscription into Russia's army, were saddened to send their sons off to war.

Lack of education and the language barrier prevented the Finland-born generation from advancing beyond barely tolerable physical work for men and caring for a brood of children for women, although women who lost a spouse or who remained single were resourceful and self-reliant enough to earn a living for themselves and their children. The second generation of Finnish Americans proved themselves as capable as any of their contemporaries; many became professionals such as attorneys, educators, architects, ministers, and engineers. Those who were unable to receive a college degree worked diligently in occupations that provided increased advantages for the third generation.

The second generation most likely married those with Finnish parentage, since they congregated together in schools and churches and thus found a commonality. Yet it was rare among the third generation to have a spouse of pure Finnish lineage, and the fifth generation may have as many as six different nationalities among their ancestors.

Elviira (Elvera) Sofia Koski Cherney

My maternal grandmother's name was Pakkala; that was her married name, but she was a widow when she came over to this country with her daughter, who was my mother, Hildur Sofia Pakkala. My mother was born in 1893, and I think she was around seventeen when they came over, so that would have been around 1910. My grandfather was Matt Myllakoski, and I know he was born in Vaasa because I have his document where he disavows his allegiance to Czar Nicholas II of Russia. My grandmother's name was Helena, and I believe they were already married when they came to this country.

My mother worked in Bjerstedt's Bakery in Ashtabula Harbor when she first arrived. And my father, Frank Einar, was a laborer on the Lake Erie docks when he met and married my mother. But he had begun sailing on the Great Lakes' boats when he was only thirteen, and he sent all his pay home to his mother.

Years later, when my father had his own business, he shortened Myllakoski to Koski. I was their fourth-born child. I was born on November 21, 1920. My two older sisters were Laura and Edith, and our brother was named Frank Edward. When it was time for me to be born, my father wanted my mother to go to the maternity hospital on Oak Street [West Eighth], but my mother refused and I was born in their house on Ontario Street [West Ninth—west of Lake Avenue].

I lost my christening certificate from the Finnish National Evangelical Lutheran church, but my name on it was Elviira Sofia Susanna Koski. I'm sure I was christened shortly after I was born because the Lutheran church subscribed to the belief that every human being was born with original sin and that it was important to have a baby baptized as soon as possible for the child to be holy and sacred. My birth certificate from the city health department spelled it: Elvira Sofia Koski, then I later changed the spelling of my first name to Elvera. My nickname is Eppie.

We went to the Harbor Special Schools, and Laura, the oldest, was the first to learn English. The teachers had to teach a great many children how to speak English, and that was quite a job. I was the youngest, and they'd have to crack down on me because I wanted my mother. They said I had tantrums because she wasn't there.

I was confirmed at age fifteen in the old Zion Lutheran Church. From my mother's point of view, our social life was entirely involved with the church. She often invited the pastor for dinner. She set the table with a damask cloth and Haviland china that she ordered from the Jewel Tea Company. At the church's women's group, she gave religious readings with much expression.

My dad had always used the sauna, but we didn't have one at our home. My experience with the sauna was we'd go to Matt Johnson's cottage on Lake Road. They had a sauna on the hillside, and we used to go to the sauna there.

I slept in a homemade crib in my parents' bedroom. I remember one night I heard my father get up and get dressed. Then he left, because he could see from our front windows that our neighbor's barn was on fire and he went to help. I remember they told me I once swallowed an open safety pin, and my grandmother fished it out from my throat. I tried ironing a doll's dress once and left the iron on. Mother was displeased when it burned the ironing board. We had a handrail supporting the upper stair railing, and I inadvertently dropped our little kitty from my hands. It fell to the lower floor, blinding it. We didn't have any more kittens after that!

My favorite store was a confectionery called Quirk's. For a nickel we could get Necco wafers, a Hershey candy bar, or an ice-cream cone—one dip. There is a family restaurant—The Lakeway—on that site now. It's decorated with nautical wallpaper, and one wall has a mural of the harbor painted on it.

My dad adored fish. He would go and get fresh fish from the fish house and bring it home. He fried it in the basement because we had a little stove down there to do the laundry with—you know, those big copper boilers to boil the linens and things in, and big enough to use for cooking. He did it downstairs so the smell wouldn't be too bad upstairs.

I remember our first automobile was an Essex with a leather top and isinglass windows. We later had a Maxwell coupe that had a box built inside to hold the crank and other tools. Dad arranged for a two-car garage to be built on our property in 1924. We also had a radio, and I remember listening to reports of Charles Lindbergh's 1927 transatlantic flight and the campaign speeches of Herbert Hoover and Alfred Smith during their 1928 campaigns.

My mother usually cooked us oatmeal for breakfast, and she made a lot of pot-roast dinners. Steak was unknown to most Finnish people because it was too expensive. When we went to play in a nearby woods, Mother would send us along with Mason jars of water and slices of bread spread with butter and brown sugar.

My mother died just short of her thirty-sixth birthday. I was eight years old then. She was very heavy and had had gall bladder surgery. They don't know if a clot hit her heart or what, but she died quite suddenly. Since our harbor bungalow wasn't large enough to accommodate a live-in housekeeper, my father moved us to a larger house on Prospect Avenue in the "uptown area." One of our first housekeepers was Lila Niemi who came from a large Finnish family.

My dad's company, Koski Construction Company, was incorporated in 1922. [Koski Construction remains at present with its earth-moving and street-paving equipment.] My dad didn't remarry until his children had all left home to marry or to attend college.

During my high-school years, I worked for the neighbors. I washed dishes, especially after they had a party, and did other household chores. I also did babysitting, and I worked as a clerk in a five- and ten-cent store. I worked in the office of my dad's company, too, but I didn't get paid.

I graduated in 1938 from Ashtabula High School. I then went to Western College for Women in Oxford, Ohio, spent one year at Ohio University, and then earned my bachelor's degree.

When I married John Sheldon in 1942 he was a flight instructor in the U.S. Naval Reserves. I went with him to bases in Kansas and Minnesota, but when he was sent to Corpus Christi there was no available housing, so I couldn't go. Then, when he was transferred to Florida, I was able to join him again. In Florida he taught guys how to land planes on an aircraft carrier. I knew we were in the South, because all the restaurants featured southern cooking.

After World War II we moved back to Ashtabula and started our family. David was born in 1946, followed by Jim, Julie, Dan, and Susan. John bought into Koski Construction and became co-owner and office manager. When our children were ages four to sixteen, John died. He was only forty-two years old then in 1962. So I went back to work. I worked in the advertising department of Carlisle's [department store], at Koski Construction, and at the *Star Beacon* again. I had worked there as a reporter before I was married.

My second husband, Andrew Cherney, was an attorney. He heard through my son's fraternity friend that I was widowed and living in Ashtabula. Andy remembered me from our school days, so he came to visit. We were married in 1969. Andy was living in Hamilton, Ohio, so I moved there, bringing my two youngest children with me, Dan and Susan. My three older kids were in college at that time. Andy and I were married only eight years when he died of cancer in 1977. I came back to Ashtabula, where I worked as a substitute teacher for six years at State Road Elementary School. I also did substitute teaching at Harbor High School and Ashtabula High School. I lived on Westminster Drive in Saybrook Township for many years before moving into an apartment at Country Club Retirement Campus.

Elvera died on September 21, 2005, two months shy of her eighty-fifth birthday. She had been a member of Women's Fortnightly Club, the Elks Ladies Association, and the Finnish-American Heritage Association. She is survived by her two daughters, three sons, fifteen grandchildren, thirteen great-grandchildren, and her sister, Laura Burchard. Elvera is buried in Chestnut Grove Cemetery, Ashtabula Township.

Elvi Aarnio Herlevi

My father's name was Johan Alpo Aarnio, and my mother's was Amanda Marie Salmi. They left Voikka, Finland, and went to Cleveland because my mother's sister, Anna Fagerholm, was living there. My parents were married in Cleveland in March of 1910 and then went to Ashtabula. They first lived upstairs of a store on the corner of West Forty-fourth Street and Station Avenue.

My father worked for the Finnish Cooperative Grocery store on Oak Street, so they moved upstairs of this store. I was born on August 22, 1910, but didn't have any brothers or sisters. They told me later that I had a half-sister in Finland.

I grew up in Ashtabula and went to the schools in the Harbor. My mother made traditional Finnish foods like meat and potato stew, salmon loaf, and meatballs. We went to meetings and social activities at Torps Hall and the Yellow Hall. My father was once treasurer of the exercise club at Sovinto Hall. He collected five-cents a week from each customer. We also went to Fourth of July and Labor Day celebrations at Sovinto. I remember "being in the way" sometimes at these gatherings when I was a child.

I took piano lessons for three years from Mrs. Mundy, but I played mostly by ear. I played with the Hani-Salo Dance Orchestra for twenty years, beginning when I was sixteen. We played Saturday nights at Torps and Wednesday night in summer at the Yellow Hall. We also played in Warren and Cleveland. I played piano accompaniment for the Sovinto Male Chorus many times, especially on holidays. [At the time of Elvi's Interview, she donated a 1934 photograph of this chorus, in their new uniforms, to the Finnish-American Heritage Association.]

One time I went with a musical group to perform in Detroit. Three cars were traveling together and the lead car slid off a bridge into the river. Some farmers rescued them, then took the people home and hung their wet clothes on the clothesline to dry. Jennie Utti had the lead part in the play, but she wasn't able to sing, once we got there, so a Detroit singer, Fannie Ojanpaa, had to be brought in to replace Jennie.

I remember how the town gathered together to give the Humina Band a big send-off when they left for their Finland Concert Tour in 1927. Then we gathered again to welcome them home in September.

I remember many of the Finnish stores throughout Ashtabula Harbor, like the cooperative grocery and mercantile stores. And there was Laine's Creamery, Kuivinen Dry Goods, Huhta Confectionary, and Erik Helander Pharmacy.

I was a 1926 graduate of Harbor High School, and we were the first class to have an outdoor commencement at Wenner Field. I was a charter member of Harbor's National Honor Society. One year the society spring-cleaned the high school during Easter vacation so we could save the school some money.

After graduation, I worked fifteen years as secretary to Harbor High's superintendent, Dr. William E. Wenner. During the Depression years, I helped my parents: I worked weekends at Roselawn Tavern [piano playing], did babysitting, clerked in grocery stores, and played piano for Finnish dances. In April 1939, all the school employees got a forty-dollar check, but we had to wait until July, when tax money was available, before we got the rest of our annual salary.

I married Carl Herlevi in 1937 after a seven-year courtship. In 1940 we bought a house with four acres on Carpenter Road. Our two children were born then: Judy, in 1943, and Tom, in 1946. We raised chickens and pigs, and we had a big vegetable garden. We had a large strawberry patch and sold 500 quarts each year. We also delivered eggs twice a week. One year we experimented with raising turkeys, and we tried raising beagle puppies.

Carl worked on the railroad during World War II. He had many extra calls and long hours so he was exempted from the draft. I helped issue applications for ration stamp books for gasoline, meat, and sugar during those years, and I registered men who were beyond the draft age but who could be called if the draft age was extended.

While the children were growing up, I was secretary for the Washington Elementary School Principal in 1958–59. Then, in the fall of 1959, I was transferred to the new Thomas Jefferson Elementary School and stayed there as a secretary for the next eleven years. So I had a total of twenty-seven years working at the Harbor schools.

We had been married forty-three years when Carl died in 1980. We were members of Bethany Lutheran and I worked on several committees there over the years. I volunteered many years, too, with the food pantry at Faith Lutheran Church, and was a volunteer at the Ashtabula County Medical Center for twenty-six years.

In December 1996, at the Light the Harbor Christmas Tree ceremony, Elvi was honored as an excellent example of a Harbor High School graduate who had dedicated most of her adult years to working and serving her community. At the age of ninety-six, Elvi now lives in an assisted-living apartment in Mentor, Ohio.

Maynard Miles Mickelson

My father, Anton Mickelson, came to this country as a teenager during the 1890s with his brother John. I don't know their original Finnish name, but my dad changed it to Mickelson after he came here. I don't know the name of the town in Finland where he came from, either, but I remember hearing him say that they traveled on one ship from Finland to England. Then when they got off the ship in England, they got lost. Somehow they made their way to the right ship and got to the United States all right.

My mother, Eviliina Putkonen, was born in Virtasalmi and came to Ashtabula in 1912 because she had a sister here who sponsored her. My mother went by Evelyn in this country. She met my dad in Ashtabula, and they were married in 1914. They first lived on West Ninth Street, in one of the houses that Kinnunen built. Then they moved to a house on West Fourteenth Street, and they lived there when I was born.

My brother, Paul Robert, was born in 1915; my brother, Arvid Anton, in 1917; and my sister, Marion Edith, in 1921. I was born April 14, 1926. We belonged to Bethany Lutheran Church.

My dad was a baker at Weichert Bakery on Main Street. Then in 1930, when I was only four years old, my dad was killed in an automobile accident.

My parents' house was already paid for when my father died, so my mother couldn't get any assistance from the government. She had done domestic work when she first came to America, so she went back to doing housework for people. She later married Charles Waris.

We went to Washington Elementary School and then to Harbor High School. During my sophomore year, I was a guard on the football team. During my senior year, I was the team quarterback. We were undefeated that year. I also played baseball and softball. During the winter I played hockey and went skiing and ice-skating. There was a pond about two miles from where I lived, so my friends and I would walk through the deep snow to get there and then clear off a place so we could play hockey. We would run water down Hubbard Hill to make it really fast and slippery. You could ride a sled all the way out to the break wall down that hill. We'd get a long toboggan that could seat about twelve people and go down the hill. Once, one of the girls got hit by a toboggan and broke her leg.

During the seventh grade, I played the trumpet. Then I fell off my bike and banged up my lip and couldn't play trumpet anymore. Then I had to play the tuba.

Sometimes we would go down to the lake and swim at Walnut Beach or Lake Shore Park; that was a good place to meet girls. We used to swim in a sulfur spring, too, that was located in an abandoned brickyard. The water there was greenish and very deep. It wasn't somewhere you should go if you didn't know how to swim, but we liked to go there because the water warmed up sooner than the water in Lake Erie. If we forgot our bathing suits, that didn't matter, we'd strip naked and dive in anyway. When we went to the public sauna, you could always tell who forgot their bathing suits by their all-over tan. I usually went to the sauna on West Eighth on Wednesday and Friday evenings. I remember the contest to see who could sit on the highest bench and withstand the most heat. Then after a bath, I would pay a quarter for a bottle of *kalja* [an unfermented beer]. And coffee—gee, I grew up on it. My mother was a good cook and she always made that coffee bread and other Finnish foods.

My first job was as a greenhouse worker. Then I worked at the Harbor shipyards during the summer between my junior and senior years of high school. I got hurt there once during a big explosion and was in the hospital for a couple of weeks. No one was killed, but lots of people were hurt. I was burned from the elbows down. It was one of the quickest haircuts I ever got!

After my high school graduation, I was in the navy from 1944 to 1946. I was on the destroyer, the USS *Kalk,* as a radio operator, and I've been an amateur radio operator ever since. Both my brothers served in World War II. Paul was an army paratrooper who was captured by the Germans on D-Day in Normandy. Then he was taken as a prisoner of war and wasn't released until the war ended in 1945.

I attended Miami [Ohio] University for a while, then I married Janet Nelson in 1952. We had six kids: David, Paul, Nancy, Amy, Jeffrey, and Eric. I worked at Reliance Electric in Ashtabula, and we lived on Elk Drive. In 1964, we moved to California, where I worked as an air-quality technician for Los Angeles County. Janet was working in a hospital when the 1971 earthquake hit, and she was killed.

I retired from my California job in 1988 and, by then, I had remarried Shirley Eklund Patterson.

Maynard's later years were spent in Tarpon Spring, Florida, with frequent visits to his hometown of Ashtabula, where he became a trustee in the Finnish-American Heritage Association and renewed acquaintances with old friends. Maynard died in his Tarpon Springs home at the age of seventy-eight on August 16, 2004.

Lina Kirkkomaki (Hill) Smith

My mother's name was Maria Hokkanen, and she was born in Karstula on October 26, 1882. My father's name was Johan Kirkkomaki, and he was born in Soini on July 16, 1882. They met when my mother's father decided to build a barn. He inquired around and found that the best barn-builder lived in Soini. His name was David Kirkkomaki, and he came with his seventeen-year-old son, Johan. The Kirkkomakis stayed there the whole summer working on the barn, and during that time my father and my mother fell in love and were married in 1900 when they were both eighteen.

My father built a small house for them, not far from my mother's family home. He was a carpenter who built barns, small buildings, and also coffins and household furniture. But times were poor in Finland then, and they were still under Russian rule.

My father's brother, Riisto, had gone alone to the United States and had a job at the Mesabi iron mines in Minnesota, so he sent a ticket to my father in 1905, and my father went alone to America. He worked in the mines for a year and a half and then got so lonesome for his family that he went back to Finland. When he found things hadn't improved there [economically], he went a second time to America. He worked for another year or so and then sent tickets to my mother and the children so they could join him. My mother left Finland, but when she got to Hull, England, the children developed a heat rash and the English thought it was a communicable disease and they put them in quarantine. Mother wasn't able to speak or understand English, so she was sent back to Finland and lost her ticket money.

Mother wrote to Father to explain what happened, and he had to work another year and a half to get enough money. Then he surprised them by coming back to Finland in April 1912. Then a bigger surprise—he had tickets for them on the *Titanic*! But they left my sister, Anna, who was ten years old, and my brother Wiljo, age six, with my grandparents. My uncle was supposed to bring these two with him later on. So my brother, Charles, who was only three, was the only one who went with my parents. What happened next was that their ship from Finland to Southhampton, England, developed engine trouble. By the time they got to England, the *Titanic* had sailed just one hour before. Anyway, they were put on the next ship, the *Empress of Britain*, and they sailed to Halifax. From there they got transportation to Minnesota without even knowing that the *Titanic* had sunk.

When they finally got to the boarding house where my father had lived before, the woman looked out the window and said, "Here comes John Hill's [anglicized name] ghost!" Another woman standing next to her said, "Then who's the woman carrying the small child with him?" Finally, they realized John Hill hadn't lost his life on the *Titanic*, after all.

My brother Toivo was born the following December. A year later, when my mother was pregnant again, they got word from Finland that Wiljo had died of a mastoid infection. My mother took to her bed in grief, so Father sent a ticket for my sister, Anna. And she traveled from Finland all alone at the age of twelve. My brother William was born that September, then a year or two later my mother had Martha Helen, but she lived only three days. I was born on August 17, 1917, in Taconite, Minnesota. I was baptized by a Reverend Niemi after my mother wrote to him to explain there was no established Lutheran church in the area where we lived. That was one of the reasons my folks decided to move to Ohio, and because they heard there was a lot of work there and that the churches were already established.

We moved first to Fairport Harbor and lived there not quite a year because work wasn't that plentiful. When my father heard there was work at the shipyards in Ashtabula Harbor, we moved there and lived in an apartment on Oak Street for about a year. After that, they bought a house on Atlantic Street, which is West Thirteenth Street today. I remember the roads were cinder covered and so were the sidewalks. My father made us wooden sidewalks. We had a barn, a cow, and black Minorca chickens, like many of the neighbors. There was a field where we could tie cows out during the summer months.

I started school at the Washington Elementary building, and half of us kids didn't know English, but it wasn't long before we learned.

Then my mother got "farm fever." She began searching south of Ashtabula and found a farm to rent on Perry Road, north of Jefferson. Most of the kids in our one-room school were Polish and Finnish. In the spring, when the ice floes started to move on Mill Creek, the boys would go up to the creek and the teacher had a terrible time getting them back in. One time they never did come back to school.

We lived on the rented farm about one year, then my folks bought a forty-acre farm on Netcher Road, east of Jefferson. The farmhouse was so run-down that the first thing my father built was steps so we could get in and out of the house. Then he built our sauna, and that's where my mother did the washing, because that's where the well was.

But my father was not a farmer. It was Mother who milked the cows and took care of the chickens, and my brothers did the field work. They planted corn, oats, and mostly hay. They would cut the hay down and rake it into little haycocks, and then Mother and I would help pitch it onto the wagon. We had horses to pull a wagon, but we didn't even have a pulley to help [lift the hay into the mow]. Eventually we had a silo built, and when the corn was dried enough we had silo-fillers come do the work.

Mother also raised chickens. She ordered baby chicks in the spring, and if the weather turned cool, she even slept near the chickens for fear the oil lamp would go out. She had two sheep, and she sheared the wool and then spun it into yarn on her spinning wheel. She also had a loom where she made her own rag rugs. Mother was a very social person. Whenever any new Finns moved into the area, she was the first to go and visit them. She liked to go visiting a lot.

My father worked for Laird Construction Company who built schools throughout a five-county area. If he had to go as far as Portage County, he would be gone all week and Mother was alone with us kids.

During summers we spent most of our spare time at Mill Creek in our swimming hole. And we picked blackberries in Wolcott's woods, which was hundreds of acres and just filled with blackberry bushes. Mother would give us a ten-quart pail to fill. Then we went along the railroad tracks and picked wild strawberries, too.

We made our own entertainment. In the evening, sometimes the Moisio kids would come over and we would play duck on the rock, Washington, hide-and-go-seek, and all kinds of games. If we were lucky enough to have a quarter, we would walk to the Ames Theatre, in Jefferson, where admission was ten cents. Isaly's dairy store was next to the theater, and ten cents would buy an ice-cream soda or a sundae or a big bag of penny candy.

I went to a one-room school for seven years. Then they built the high school in Jefferson for the junior-high and high-school students. We rode in a kid hack, pulled by horses, and it was cold in wintertime even with straw on the floor of the wagon, and with heated stones and blankets. When there was a real lot of snow, Jesse Sharp, our driver, put sled runners on the wagon. During my last year they brought us in cars as there were no school buses yet. I graduated high school in 1935.

Then I want to tell you about our religious life. We belonged to the old Zion Lutheran Church on Joseph Avenue in Ashtabula. Because of the long distance and bad roads, we weren't able to get there much during winter, so Sunday school was out of the question. So we had our own Sunday school when we met in different homes. Alex Tokkanen was the leader, and we would have our Bible lessons around the dining-room table. Each of us older children would take turns reading the Bible lesson, then he would ask questions about it. After our lesson, there was always refreshments: coffee and *nisua* and cookies. Once a month there was a religious meeting for adults and children. We sang songs from a Finnish hymnal, had readings, and sometimes musical numbers. Of course, there were refreshments and a lot of visiting.

When any Finns had any kind of tragedy, they would all pitch in. I remember when Allemans came from Detroit and moved into Dorset. It wasn't long after that their house burned, so all the Finns got together and brought them seed for grain, a calf, and some chickens. And there were a lot of money gifts, too.

In Finland they celebrate name days instead of birthdays. A certain day of the year is your name day. A group would come and sing under your window, and, of course they were invited in for cake and coffee and *nisua*. My mother always celebrated *Juhannus*. She would drape leaves over pictures and doorways, and we would have a huge outdoor bonfire. At Christmastime we didn't get a lot of gifts. We decorated a tree with Finnish flags, and my brother would write out a banner in Finnish: "Unto us a child is born; unto us a son is given." Then the banner was draped around the tree. Father always read the lesson in Finnish, and he would read a long, long time. My brother, who was very impatient, once said, "Come on, that's enough of that!" Our gifts were an orange and some hard candy in our stocking, and my mother always knitted us some mittens. Sometimes I got a doll when I was younger, but gifts weren't a big thing. It was the idea of being together and having a feast of pork roast. On New Year's Day we had cod fish, which I didn't care for.

My mother always cooked Finnish foods. She baked her own bread and made her own butter. What I didn't like was when she cooked potatoes with sardines in it. My brother Toivo would go look in the pot and see those eyes looking back at him, then he would say we weren't going to eat tonight. So he would make us french toast instead, as he was a pretty good cook. Mother also liked to make *viilia* [yogurt-like dish made from whole milk]. She would put a tablespoon of starter [culture] in and add fresh, warm milk. One time she ran out of starter, so she wrote to relatives in Finland for another. They sent a letter back with dried starter wrapped in cheesecloth. All you had to do was soak the cheesecloth in warm milk and you had the starter again.

When Anna came to America at age twelve, she had to start in the first grade until she learned English. Then they skipped her into the right age group. When she was sixteen she won the State of Minnesota's spelling contest, but Dad was old-fashioned and he wouldn't let her go to the national contest in San Francisco. So she quit school and got a job in a nearby hospital, working as a nurses' aid. Since she hadn't been to confirmation school, she was sent to Fairport Harbor and stayed with some friends so she could attend. Anna later worked on a Great Lakes' liner as a chambermaid. She married Herman Kotila.

Charlie, at age six, had osteomyelitis [bone inflammation] and went to St. Paul Hospital, where they removed two toes. Then again, when he was around fourteen, he got it again in his hip. He went to Elyria Memorial Hospital, and he was there one and a half years. They removed his hip bone, and he was in a cast from his waist to knees. He was sent there by the Rotary Club, and A.J. Kane was his sponsor. Charlie was a talented artist, and Kane offered to send him to an art school in Cleveland, but Father wouldn't let him go. We were living on the Perry Road farm when Charlie came back home, a cripple. He never married, and died at age forty-five.

Toivo married Eleanor Tikkonen from the Harbor and was in the army during World War I. Brother Bill was in the army, too, and during the Depression they both worked in CCC camps. Toivo went to the Mount Shasta, California, area, clearing forests. Bill went to Peninsula [Ohio] to help build a park. Bill married Hilma Jarmii from North Dakota. Everyone in my family married a Finn except me!

After high school, I got to go to Finland for a year. Zion Lutheran Church sponsored me to go to People's College in Karkku, Finland. I took regular classes, plus homemaking classes, like cooking and baking. I learned more Finnish language, too, and some of the old traditions. When I got back, I found a job in Jefferson.

Then one day a friend arranged for me to have a blind date with Ithiel Smith, but everyone called him Ike. So he picked me up with his car, and we went to a movie in Ashtabula, and then went across the street for an ice-cream sundae. Then he dropped me off at home and I thought: "Well, that's the end of that!" But then a couple days later, a knock came on the door and my mother said, "There's a young man here to see you." There was Ike. He wanted me to go "Halloweening" with him. His car had corn stalks tied to the running board and we drove all over Jefferson that night.

So then we got married on February 8, 1939, in the old Zion Lutheran Church in Ashtabula Harbor when Reverend G. A. Aho was pastor.

In 1942 we found a ninety-acre farm in Richmond Township that was for sale. They wanted a $280 down payment, but we didn't have enough and had to borrow $200 to buy it. We had three girls by that time. Mary Lou was three years old; Sally was two; and Bonnie only three months. It wasn't much of a place then. We had to carry all our water, and we had an outside toilet. No furnace—just a cook stove in the kitchen and a wood-burning heating stove in the living room. The kitchen was painted a funny brown color, and the roof leaked, so Ike nailed an old mattress to the ceiling.

Ike worked at a box factory in Ashtabula at first, and he earned forty cents an hour. I had one more baby, too—another girl, Linda. We were on that farm almost thirty-five years, and it was in good condition when we left it. We retired from farming in 1977 and moved to a smaller house on Clay Street and later moved to an apartment in Jefferson.

Ike and I had been married fifty-nine years when he died on October 19, 1998. But I keep busy with the church—St. Paul's Lutheran—in Jefferson; in fact, I'm a charter member. I've traveled some, and I've always been a reader.

Lina was nominated "Cook of the Week" in July 1999, and her Finnish nisua recipe was published in a local newspaper. After an extended illness, Lina died in Conneaut's Brown Memorial Hospital on December 8, 1999, at age eighty-two. She is buried in Jefferson's Oakdale Cemetery.

Ellen Edythe Salo Maxim

My father was Emil Waldemar Merisalo. He was born on August 17, 1894, in Hauho, Finland. By the time he was eighteen, employment hardly existed, so he decided to immigrate to the United States in 1913. His father, Aksel Waldemar Merisalo, loaned him 400 marks for this new venture. On June 11 he boarded the *Titania* in Hango, Finland, where he bought a ticket to New York for 263 marks. He docked in Hull, England, then went by train to Southampton. On June 18 he boarded the *Oceanic* of the White Star Line and set sail for New York.

My father made friends onboard the ship, and they assisted him in purchasing a railroad ticket to Duluth, Minnesota. In that area, he did so well working in the forests that he was able to repay his father's 400 marks. And at every opportunity he studied the English language. He also shortened his last name to Salo.

In 1916, my dad moved from Duluth to Cleveland, where there was plenty of work. He became a carpenter and, a year later, joined the carpenter's union. He had been earning forty cents an hour, but once in the union he earned seventy cents an hour.

My mother, Ellen Maria Praski, was born in Isokyro on December 16, 1893. Her father came to this country in 1900, yet my mother didn't arrive in Cleveland until 1913, when she was twenty years old. I don't know where my parents met, but they were married in Cleveland on April 16, 1917. I was born in November of that same year, when they were living on John Avenue in the Ohio City area. Although my name is Ellen Edythe, I've always been known as Edythe to avoid confusion with my mother's name, and even that has been shortened to Edy.

On October 17, 1918, my folks purchased an eighty-five-acre farm in Ashtabula County on Atkins Road in Harpersfield, south of Geneva. We had a two-story house, a barn with one cow, a garage, a chicken house, an outhouse, and, of course, a sauna. If there was space for one, Finnish people would always include a sauna. We had two vineyards there, too, and the rest of the acreage was wooded. We used kerosene lamps, and we cooked and heated with woodstoves.

When I was about two or three, I thought all fuzzy, feathery, little creatures were ducklings, so I put some of these babies into a bucket of water so they could swim. To my dismay, my mother told me these were little chickens, not ducklings; unfortunately, they drowned. Our cow laid down one night and rolled over on our cat, killing it; I felt bad about that, too. Another time, on one rainy day, my mother and I left Cleveland for Unionville on the Interurban, which operated between Cleveland and Ashtabula County. From the small village of Unionville, we still had about a five-mile walk to our farm, and the entire route was through muddy roads. En route, I recall telling my mother that I thought I had lost my rubbers in the mud. I just couldn't see them as we continued our muddy trek. However, when we reached home, I happily discovered I was still wearing them over my shoes. I never forgot my surprise.

In the beginning of the 1920s very few people owned cars; consequently, there was very little traffic. My father did have a Chevy touring car, and one road that we used frequently was State Route 534. In those years, it was exceptional to have a paved road, and on this route only one half of the road was paved with brick. The paved side was used by cars coming from either direction when traffic permitted. In other words, when our car was southbound we would move over to the unpaved side until the other car passed by, then we'd go back to the paved side.

When I was old enough to start school, we moved back to Cleveland but still kept the farm property and returned there frequently during vacation periods. I started classes in Kentucky School, which was also in the Ohio City area.

On one occasion, we were driving along Lake Shore Boulevard in Bratenahl, just east of Cleveland, on our way to the farm. It started to rain, so we stopped at Eddy Road to put in the isinglass windows on the doors of the Chevy touring car. I never heard of that type of window again until in later years when I had sports cars like the MG and the Triumph. I remember that incident so well and was surprised to discover, about ten years later, that the man I was to marry lived just opposite of the spot where we stopped.

I had a doll when we moved back into the city; however, I accidentally dropped it on the sidewalk and its head broke. I just didn't play with dolls after that, so I guess that was the start of my becoming a tomboy.

I never met my great-grandparents, yet I was fortunate to be well acquainted with my maternal grandmother, who we frequently visited. Every summer I would stay with her for two weeks in Chagrin Falls. As I grew older, during high-school days, she was a "house mother" for my sorority sisters and me when we vacationed at her farm.

I met my paternal grandparents during the summer of 1928, when I was ten years old. My parents and I visited them in Finland for three months.

It was a lovely experience to see other countries like Finland and England. I learned to speak Finnish quite well, too, and also met aunts and uncles. Women of that era were mostly homebodies, and my grandparents were retired by that time. My grandfather had been a shoemaker and, just for fun, he made me a pair of shoes. One thing Grandfather enjoyed was to go fishing. My father and I went along with him on several occasions. He used the net method of fishing with busy workers on each end of the net. When we retrieved the net we would save a small fish or two for the family cat. I called these fish "catfish," since they were for the cat, when they were really a kind of sunfish.

Our crossing to Finland was made on the *Lancastria,* that took twelve days, although the return trip from Southampton was made in five days in the largest and fastest vessel of the time, the *Mauretania.* Even more impressive was that just the year before, in 1927, Charles Lindbergh made the first transatlantic flight in thirty-three and a half hours.

In 1929 my dad began building us a house on St. James Avenue, west of Cleveland. Then the Depression years started, and he finished the house's interior a little at a time. Coal was still used for heating, which was common then. If we were gone all day, more than likely the coals were not successfully banked, and a new fire would have to be started when we returned. We had an icebox, and there was always a chance that the water catch basin beneath the icebox would overflow.

My brother, Allan Waldemar, was born on June 11, 1931. By that time, I was attending Longmead Junior High. In 1933, my father legally changed our surname to Salo when he applied for his citizenship. My mother, too, became Salo on her citizenship papers in 1943.

My class of eighty-eight students was the first to graduate from the new John Marshall High School in 1936. Ours was the January class, with forty-four girls and forty-four boys. Later that year I entered Western Reserve University in Cleveland. I met John Henry Maxim in 1937 when he was about to graduate from Case School of Applied Science. It was love at first sight, you might say, and we were engaged in September 1937. I went to college one more year, and then John and I were married on October 8, 1938.

Immediately out of college, John chose to work for General Electric Company. He was sent to various branches to get acquainted with the productions of those plants. We had three-month periods in each. When we were first married, we lived in Fort Wayne, Indiana; then Erie, Pennsylvania; and then Schenectady, New York. At that point he was hoping to get transferred to

Nela Park, in Cleveland, but there were no openings. So he left GE and we moved back home to Cleveland. John chose to go to Park Ohio Industries, where he worked until his retirement forty-two years later.

I continued my college studies by going to school six months and then working six months. During the working months, I also took night-school courses. Then World War II came into the picture, and the American Ship Building Company offered me a full-time position. I worked for them through the entire war period.

John was interested in flying, and so he and a friend made a bid on a brand-new government-owned Taylorcraft that was no longer needed for the war. Their bid was accepted, and John started flying lessons immediately. He got his pilot license a year later in 1945. I used to fly with him out of Cleveland Hopkins [Airport] as his navigator.

On August 3, 1948, my mom passed away at the young age of fifty-four. John and I sold our home and moved to Dad's home on the west side of Cleveland—the same house he built in 1929. That winter we encouraged my dad to go to Florida, where there was a community of many Finns. He did, and it was here where he met Olga Lintula Raita, a friend of theirs from years before. Olga was also a Finnish immigrant who had come to America in 1920 when she was eighteen. When Dad met her, she was living in Oneco, Connecticut, where she had a chicken farm. Dad married Olga in Oneco on June 25, 1949.

Then Allan got married and moved into our father's house, so John and I bought a home in Berea, and then later bought a larger house in North Olmsted where I would live for thirty-four years.

I started flying lessons in 1950 and received my license in 1951. I thought I should learn how to land a plane just in case it ever became necessary. In our early years of flying, our aircraft radios were low frequency, then very high frequency was developed, which made communications and navigation much simpler and safer. Over the years we owned three airplanes. The Musketeer was the last one, and I got my instrument and commercial licenses in it. Then its name went from Musketeer to Mouseketeer to Mouse. Although I no longer have my Mouse, I continue to have loving remembrances of it from my many aviation friends. Ever since I started to fly, aviation has had a special spot in my life. It has been wonderful to add aviators to my list of friends.

In 1970 I received my instrument rating, and in 1971 my commercial rating. I received quite a few awards, such as Pilot of the Year Achievement Award in 1958; Pilot of the Year Achievement Award—All Ohio Chapter in 1966; and Lake Erie Chapter in 1975. In October 1975, I was accepted as a member of the Silver

Wings Fraternity after flying solo for twenty-five years. I flew two Powder Puff Derbies, the Angel Derby, and in numerous local races. I am a charter member of the Lake Erie Chapter 99s, which had been formed in January of 1974. I was also secretary-receptionist for Sohio Aviation Service, fixed-base operation, at Cleveland Hopkins. I retired in 1978, the same year John retired.

My dad and Olga traveled to Finland to visit family and friends in 1959 and in 1962. After thirty years of marriage, Olga died in Connecticut in 1979. My dad made one more trip to Finland in 1984, then he died in 1985, shortly before his ninety-first birthday. My brother Allan then added Dad's name to the American Immigrant Wall of Honor at Ellis Island.

John and I went to Philadelphia in 1963 where he attended a convention. I spent my time shopping and seeing the sights of the city. While walking along, I became aware of a strange quietness, and noticed people were whispering. Finally, in a store, I heard someone say that President Kennedy had been shot. At that moment no one even knew that he was dead. This happened to be my forty-fifth birthday—November 22, 1963—and I shall never forget that day.

John and I had been married fifty-three years when he died in October of 1991. In early 1992 I began planning a trip to Finland. I hadn't been there for sixty-four years, and this time it was a seven-hour flight, directly from New York to Helsinki, in an MD-11 jet, a brand new type with winglets. This change in mode of travel was truly an exciting experience. The flight progress was constantly being shown on TV monitors. By the time of this visit, my grandparents were deceased, but the family encouraged me to visit the cemetery. I still had three aunts and many cousins there who showed me more of Finland than I had originally seen. My grandparents' home is now a historic site, and it isn't permitted to be altered. Other original homes, stores, the church, and the narrow roads were still the same, although the rest of the village has kept up with current trends. I had remembered that the railroad station in Helsinki had a huge twenty-four-hour clock in front of the building. I was eager to see it again, hoping it would be the same, but it wasn't. It was just a twelve-hour clock.

Dr. "Pete" Bonar came into my life in 1992. His home was in Arizona. He liked North Olmsted, but felt that winter came too soon. Thus, in 1994, I changed from one acre and a house to a condo in North Ridgeville. I'm a resident in Ohio for six months and in Arizona for six months. Even though I lost Pete in 1997, I'm still doing the same routine. I have dear friends in both states, but at times it gets lonesome.

At this time (2003), I have cousins and other relatives who are extensively researching the genealogy I already have, so we'll gain more information on both my paternal and maternal sides of the family. I hope that additional research will bring forth more information on my husband's side of the family, as well. By comparing what has happened in the past, with what has been happening in recent years, has been most interesting. It's unbelievable that so many new innovations keep coming along. I can only say to keep learning, keep watching, and keep adding to life with your ideas and actions.

Aili Hokkanen

My father, John Hokkanen, and my mother, Maria Kovonen Hokkanen, both came from Jyväskylä, Finland. In 1913 they went first to Canada, and my father got a job in a nickel mine. They lived there for less than a year, then my mother wanted them to move to northern Michigan, or Wakefield, near Ironwood, because her sister lived there. So my father quit his job and they went to live there.

I was born in Wakefield on March 29, 1914, but when I was three, my mother became sick. She couldn't stand the weather, and the doctor told her she had to move to a different climate. We were going to move to Conneaut, but my father found a job with the New York Central Railroad in Ashtabula. That was in 1916, and he later worked for the gas company. Then my mother and I came, and we lived with the Moisio family on Joseph Avenue. The Moisios were cousins, and we rented two rooms upstairs of their house.

I didn't speak a word of English when I started school at the Jackson Building. We rented places on West Fifth Street, and then Cherry Street [West Ninth], when I transferred to Washington School. I was thirteen when we bought our house on Joseph Avenue, not far from Bethany Lutheran, where we went to church. No, I never had any brothers or sisters.

We always had rutabaga on special holidays like Christmas and Thanksgiving. My mother made fish stews, baked fish, meat and potato stew, and all kinds of vegetables. My mother baked bread, and even *kalaleipä*, which is a fish bread; you could slice it and have the fish filling inside it. My father learned to bake bread, too. I used to bring his bread for the church's bake sales, and Helja Hjerpe would be waiting there on a bench when I came with the bread. She wanted to make sure she got a loaf of his bread. And we had buttermilk, *kropsua* [an oven-baked dessert pancake], and, oh—fruit soup—you can make it with cranberries or strawberries that you cook.

I remember the Yellow Hall on Lake Avenue, going uptown. They had dances, and they had plays; it was real nice. Then there was Torps Hall, which was on Joseph Avenue, and they had dancing a lot there. They had this one lady that played the accordion, Viola Turpinen, and we were told we couldn't go in there, but we stayed at the top of the hill and then we could hear the music. We used to go to the church picnics, too, and picnics at Woodman Park—the insurance people had picnics and programs there. At one time there was so much land at the end of Walnut Street that it was called a park, but now it's all eroded there. We lived next door to Sovinto Hall, and they had plays there. We would go behind the fence and listen to the Humina Band when they played there.

One time my mother told me to go and get three pounds of beef roast, only she said, *lehmä paisti,* and I didn't know how to say it the right way, so I told the butcher, "I want three pounds of cow meat." I think the people around there must have been laughing, but the butcher gave it to me. When I went home, my mother said, "That's nice." So then she got the brilliant idea that—well, since that beef roast was so good, she sent me another time for *sika paisti,* and I thought, here we go again. Anyway, I went there again, and I said, "Well, that other meat was good, so now my mother wants three pounds of pig meat." It didn't seem to be a problem, so I took it home and my mother thought it was great. Lampilas had a grocery store on West Eighth Street, and being that I was the one that went to store, and when it was payday, my mother gave me the money to pay them. In those days, if you paid your bill you would get some extra candy and bananas, so I thought that was great, and I always wanted to go pay the bill.

Talvola's Bakery had the best round skorpers [toasted sweetbread]; they were round on the bottom, like a ball, and they would probably cut it. Their butter biscuits were out of this world! Then there was Rasmus's Confectionery Store, and—oh—we thought that was great. They had an ice-cream social place in the back with round tables and wire chairs and, boy, we thought that was pretty great. I remember one time, but probably I shouldn't say it, but Mr. Hukari, he had a construction company, but then when he got late in years, he really couldn't remember things too well. I know one time I went to buy an ice-cream cone from Rasmus's, and I was coming down the street, and there was Mr. Hukari on the corner. He said, "Give me that ice-cream cone!" Well, I thought that was terrible, but he took it and ate it.

We had lots of fun growing up. We used to go down the hill near the river on our sleds, and we roller skated down the hill, too. One time I went down the hill on the sidewalk, and I got to such a momentum that by the time I got down near the laundry I turned in too quickly, and there was this mud and rain water, and I went right smack into that mud and was covered from head to toe! Everyone laughed at me.

My first job when I was in school was washing dishes for some of the teachers. When I graduated from Harbor High School in 1932, I went to work for an insurance company. Then I went to work in the hospital; I got more money there. One day I was running to catch the streetcar and I fell and couldn't get up. My friend was following me, and she said, "Well, get up!" So I finally dragged myself to the streetcar, and the driver, a Finn, Mr. Stenroos, said I'd better go back to the hospital because he thought I wasn't doing too well. But I said, "Oh no, I have to go because it's the last night of the carnival uptown." When my father came to the door at home he thought I had broken my leg, and my mother had just broken her arm the same week when she fell, so I didn't dare tell him how much it hurt, because it was the last night of the carnival and I thought that was more important. This friend of mine came and we tried to tie up my leg, and my father said I wasn't going anyplace with that, but we insisted that we had to go. We had to walk to Lake Avenue to get the streetcar, then walk all the distance uptown to Main Avenue and West Forty-sixth Street, but we did it.

During the Depression, it seemed like everybody was helping everyone else. The railroad would tell people when they would drop coal at night so they could go get it. Then our milkman said if people were willing to take the milk, because it would ruin the cows if he couldn't milk them, he would bring the milk all the Depression time, and people would say they would pay for it afterwards. Some didn't, but most of them did. So he was real happy about that. My mother used to take in sewing at that time.

During World War II, I worked second shift in a war factory. I had a friend who was a teacher, and she took a leave of absence and came to work at the factory, too. Then we used to go on a train to Cleveland to business college after work. I had an old Model A Ford, and I'd go over there and stop the car. She would run in and get the tickets and then meet me at the train. I was a caseworker for welfare a couple years while I was taking courses. I transferred to Kent State [University], when they were uptown, and then transferred to Lake Erie College and went nights there. When I got my teaching degree, I first substituted, and then taught at Happy Hearts School.

Then I did payroll at Lake City Malleable plant on State Road for ten years. At the same time I took a beauty course in Erie at night. I'd get home about 2:00 in the morning, then get up and go back to the plant and work all day. When I finished the beauty course, I had to practice for six months in Pennsylvania. That was a bad winter, and my father wouldn't let me go alone. I got a job in West Springfield as a beauty operator. So my father would wait in a beer joint because they had a TV there. We didn't have any at home in those days, you know. When I'd get through fixing the ladies' hair, we'd come home. Eventually, I started working at home in my own beauty shop, called Aili's Beauty Shop, on Joseph Avenue.

Without siblings or a family of her own, Aili was the sole caregiver of her parents during their later years. Aili currently (2005) resides at the Park Haven Home in Ashtabula and is ninety-one years old.

Robert Willehad Nieminen

Robert Willehad Nieminen was born in Joutsa, Finland, on December 22, 1890. His parents were Roope and Amalia Nieminen, and he had at least one older brother, Viktor, and a younger sister, Lydia Aleksandra.

Robert saw some of the country outside his home parish. For a while his family worked herding horses into Lapland, possibly for use in the logging industry. Robert was the only one in his immediate family to emigrate from Finland. As a middle child, his chance of taking over the family farm was slim. Perhaps he wanted to flee hardship and poverty there, or maybe he didn't want to be conscripted into the Russian army. Years later, his son claimed that Robert hated Russians. He associated the color red with Russians, and he would never wear anything red. And he used to talk about the terrible things the Russians did to the Finns. In any event, he began making plans to leave Finland for America.

Family legend claims that Robert intended to sail on the ill-fated *Titanic* in 1912 but got drunk and missed the boat that was to carry him from Sweden to England. Nieminen descendents haven't been able to prove whether this yarn is fact or fable, but it is known that he came to the United States on the *Lusitania* in 1914, when he was twenty-four years old. He didn't speak any English, and he had only a few dollars in his pocket.

After the required inspections at Ellis Island, Robert caught a train west and got off in Ohio, most likely at the old railroad depot in Conneaut. From there, he traveled on to the farming community of Williamsfield, in southern Ashtabula County. There he got a job in a sawmill and lived in a shack in the woods where there was, at least, a well with a hand pump.

Although Robert might have been homesick upon his initial arrival, it didn't take him long to find a niche in the new land. Rural Williamsfield had a small Finnish population, and he eventually got to know some of the other area Finns. The Frabacks were one of the Finnish American families he first became acquainted with. The Frabacks operated a large dairy farm, and Robert got a job there as a farmhand. And it was there that he met his future bride, Senia Maria Fraback. Senia was the daughter of Finnish immigrants Juha (John) Erkki (Erik) and Maria Loviisa Kinnunen Fraback. Senia was two years younger than Robert and had been born on March 14, 1892, in Ashtabula Harbor. She was the oldest of fourteen children.

Robert and Senia courted for a year or so before marrying, and one amusing story about their courtship has been handed down through the generations. One evening when Robert came to call, some of Senia's devious younger brothers decided it would be good fun to stand in front of an open upstairs window and urinate down on the love-struck couple who were seated below. Even this prank didn't discourage Robert, for he married Senia on April 14, 1916.

Robert and Senia's only child, Elmer Robert Niemi, was born June 27, 1917, when they lived on a California Road farm in Williamsfield. They later moved to Andover, where Robert built a house along South Pymatuning Lake Road near the Pymatuning Lake's main beach. The house was built from scrap lumber salvaged from homes that were torn down when Mosquito Creek in Trumbull County was flooded to make Mosquito Lake. It was Elmer who later shortened the Nieminen surname to Niemi, making it easier to pronounce and to spell. Nieminen and Niemi are two of the more common surnames in Finland. Nieminen means "little cape," and Niemi means "cape," and sometime over the years, Robert Willehad became known simply as "Bill."

In addition to farming and carpentering, Bill worked as a truck driver. He transported livestock to and from Cleveland prior to the Great Depression. He also camped in the woods, days at a time, while working as a logger near Chardon, Ohio.

Although Bill learned to speak English quite well, he never became a United States citizen. He retained many Finnish traditions, such as bathing weekly in a sauna and drinking lots of coffee with salt in it. He liked to pick berries, and he subscribed to a Finnish American newspaper. When he became annoyed with something, he proclaimed, "I go back to ol' country!" Yet he never returned to Finland, nor did he see his parents or siblings again. He learned of his mother's death in 1922 and his father's in 1929 from letters received in black-edged envelopes.

Bill once collapsed on the ground and Senia rushed to his side, pounding frantically on his chest. Her quick action most likely saved him from a mild heart attack. He was not as fortunate, however, when he went to an Andover barbershop one day. While seated in a chair, waiting to have his hair cut, he quietly slumped over following a massive, and fatal, heart attack.

Robert Willehad Nieminen died at the age of sixty-seven on July 5, 1958. He is buried in Andover's Maple Grove Cemetery next to his wife and their son, Elmer, who died in 2001.

Rebecca Niemi Sloan contributed these accounts of her great-grandfather's life.

Aarne E. Roivas

My mother, Aino Antilla, was born in Orivesi, Finland, April 2, 1894. She came from a family of eleven children, and her parents were Emanuel and Kustaava Antilla. My father's name was Mikko Roivas, and he married my mother in 1914. They left Finland in 1916, and it was a hard trip to come here. Because it was during the middle of World War I, they couldn't go through the North Sea or the Baltic Sea because the Germans had mined them. Instead, they had to go by train to Oulu, in northern Finland, and then go into Norway and sail from there.

Once they got to Liverpool, England, they finally boarded a ship for the United States. The ship was turned back after only two days at sea because the British thought there was German contraband aboard. So they were delayed a couple days in Liverpool before the ship was allowed to continue on again. This was in February and there were winter storms. Then, because of the delay in Liverpool, the ship ran out of food three days before it arrived at Ellis Island. All they had left was milk and onions, so they made soup from that for those last days.

My mother was pregnant with me at that time, and the officials at Ellis Island held them up there because they were afraid my mother wouldn't make the trip to Ashtabula before I was born. Anyway, they finally let them go, and I was born three weeks after my folks got to Ashtabula. My birth date is March 13, 1916, and they were living on Parsons Street [a section of West Thirty-eighth Street] then. My brother Leo was born the next year on the Fourth of July, 1917, and we were the only kids they had. We lived in a duplex when Leo was born—on Lake Avenue, across from the Smith Memorial sales' place. Then, a year or so later, they bought a house on East Twenty-third Street. My father worked several places, and he also found places for people who came from Finland. He worked at the Ashtabula Hide and Leather [a tannery], then from there he went to the shipyards where he and his brother painted boats. Then he worked on the New York Central for a while.

One of my uncles had been to this country before my folks came. When he went back to Finland, he said that in Finland you don't see any money ever, but when you're in Ashtabula at least you see money every two weeks.

World War I lasted till 1918, and then we got the flu epidemic. I lost my godmother, Julia Ruuska, in that. I still remember her. She used to have painted dogs in those days, made out of chalk, and one dog had glass eyes. I always had to climb the stairs to go see that dog. Pretty soon I couldn't go over there because of the flu.

In 1923, we moved to Waynesburg, Pennsylvania, south of Pittsburgh. I went my first six grades in school there. My teacher in the first grade said I couldn't spell my name with double *a*'s, so I had to drop one of the *a*'s in Aarne, but that's the way it's spelled on my birth certificate. My dad was working in the coal mines there, and in 1926 he bought a new Model-T Ford. By the time I was twelve, I was driving that car.

I remember the mine explosion on May 19, 1928, when a lot of Finns lost their lives. They were having problems with the mine, starting at eleven in the morning before lunch. The ventilation system gave out and the gas accumulated in there and it blew up. But my dad happened to come home early that day, and he never did that before, so he missed it. Some of the Finns who got killed had just moved there from the Sugar Creek, Ohio, area. Anyway, that's when my folks decided to move back to Conneaut. We were there about one year, and then moved to Ashtabula again. We moved around so much in the 1920s and 1930s that our family Bible got lost. It had names and dates in it, and I sure regret losing it. We lost other things, too, because it was hard to haul stuff without a truck in those days.

My folks subscribed to at least three Finnish newspapers: the *Raivaaja*, the *Amerikan Uutiset*, and the *Eteenpain*. They kept up on politics to see what was going on. My mother had only four years of schooling, but she could read Finnish real well, and some Swedish, so she managed to write real good articles for these newspapers.

I helped my mother take care of our one cow and the chickens, and we had a pet cat. That area around East Twenty-third was full of Finns and Italians, and they kept cows. I remember getting an ice-cream cone from a guy selling them from his horse-drawn wagon. They cost three or five cents in those days. They used to deliver groceries with a horse and wagon, too. The main guy's name was Arnio, and he'd start at the Harbor and circle around and go all the way uptown, then to the west side, and back to the Harbor.

The first time my mother had to go to the Cleveland Clinic we traveled by streetcar all the way. It started from Center and Main streets, through Madison, and all the way to downtown Cleveland. Then we had to backtrack to East Ninety-first Street on Euclid. Another streetcar had to let us off on Ninety-third. We didn't take a train because we were short on the language; that's going back to the early 1920s.

During the summers of 1933 and 1934—the Depression years—I worked at Griswold Greenhouse for ten cents an hour. When I tell that to kids nowadays, they laugh at me.

After my graduation from Harbor High School in 1935, I went to Ohio Northern to get my electrical engineering degree. A group of seven of us from Harbor went to the same college. Before and during World War II, I worked in radar research at Wright Field—near Dayton—and finally got my degree in 1943. I worked on radars and transmitters for airplanes for eight years. Then I went to Raytheon Corporation in Chicago, then to Boston. Raytheon developed aimed radar signals that are still used today.

I got married in 1950 when I was thirty-four years old. People would ask me why I wanted to get married then; they thought I wouldn't live long enough to see my children graduate. And I told them that maybe I'd see my grandchildren, and their grandchildren. My wife Elizabeth (Betty) already had a daughter, Cecilia, then we had Michael in 1952 and then Susan. We lived on Hallwood, off Lake Road West, in Ashtabula.

I worked for my cousins, Edwin and Ahti Roivas. They owned a small engine repair business on Lake Avenue. We serviced engines for industries and for individuals. This business was known as Roivas Motors until Ed died in the mid-1960s, then it was renamed Mid-City Electric. I was their engineer who did the troubleshooting and helped them correct problems. After Mid-City was sold, I worked ten years as an electrician for A & B Docks, and I retired from there.

My father had died in 1954, and my mother spent her later years in the Ashtabula Care Center. They had a party for her there when she reached 100. I used to visit her at least twice a day, and I think that helped keep her alive.

She lived to be 104. My brother Leo was in the Carington Park Home, and he died in 2000, at age eighty-two. Leo graduated from Ohio Northern, too, in 1941. He was a civil engineer for several companies, but mostly at Bethlehem Steel in Cleveland.

My daughter Susan and I went to Finland in 2001. We rented a place in Mikkeli because I wanted to avoid staying with relatives. We rented a new Volvo and drove all the way to the Russian border. Those guards over there spoke Finnish, not Russian, and when I spoke to one guard, he said he knew right away I was from Karelia, because my folks always had that Karelian dialect. Sortavala, where my dad's folks came from, is on the Russian side now. We met four cousins on my mother's side of the family, and I have a handwritten ancestral record book that's five hundred years old. By reading this I was able to trace some of my relatives in Finland. I bought myself a computer and learned to use it, then I traced some Roivases in the States. Roivas means "a ball of flax thread." My ancestors owned the largest flax farm in Finland.

In the summer of 2002, my daughter and I visited the Delaware Valley site where the Finns and Swedes established their first colony in 1638. We saw the oldest surviving wooden structure, the 1654 birthplace of John Morton. Morton descends from these early Finnish settlers, and he was the last one to sign the Declaration of Independence. He was a delegate from Pennsylvania. We took pictures of the old log home and of Morton's gravesite. Morton Drive in Ashtabula Harbor is named after that same Morton.

I discovered I had knee trouble and had to give up skiing in Colorado. My son and daughter always went there. I had knee surgery in 1998, so I hope my knees will last for a while.

At age eighty-nine (2005), Aarne lives independently in an Ashtabula apartment.

Verna J. Warpula

I was born in Mustasaari, Finland, on April 12, 1911. My father's and mother's names were Henry and Sanna (Myllymaki) Warpula. I had one brother, Weikko Warpula. My father wanted to come to the United States in 1917 because he didn't want to get drafted in the Russian army, so we left when I was six years old. I can still remember the terrible storm we had when we were on the boat from Vaasa to Sweden. It was frightening! And the only people on deck were the captain and an old nurse. I can't remember the name of the ship that sailed us across the Atlantic, but I do remember how cramped we were in those third-class cabins and how seasick I was.

We came to Conneaut and rented a house on Buffalo Street. My father got a job with the Nickel Plate Railroad. Then, in 1922, my father wanted to go back to Finland because he thought he might be able to get the old family farm back. By then the war was over, so he wasn't worried about having to go into the army.

After we moved back to Finland, my parents, my brother, and I lived in an apartment in Vaasa. Not much conflict with Russia had taken place in Vaasa, but I remember there was a lady living in our apartment building who was from the eastern part of Finland, and she told us that the Russians came and took her husband one night and she never saw him again.

I went to school in Vaasa—Vaasa *Yhteis Koulu*—when it was just getting started. Today they have a big, beautiful school building there. I saw it again when I visited in 1980.

Then my father found out that times were even harder in Finland than they had been in America. At that time in Finland there was a lot of poverty and not much work, so back we came again just a year later in 1923. This time my dad bought a big dairy farm on Hatches Corners Road in Monroe Township [south of Conneaut].

There were other Finn families in Monroe, and we all used to go to weddings, dances, and plays in the farmers' hall on the corner of our road and Route 7. We went to Kilpi Hall, too, in Conneaut. Kilpi Hall was built in 1899, and now it's the Conneaut Community Center. My dad acted in some of the plays there, and he played the clarinet in the Kilpi Band. I have a picture of him with that band. We went there on Fourth of July, and for Finnish holidays, like *Juhannus*, and we went there on New Year's Eve, too. There was a superstition we used to do then. You poured hot lead into a pot of cold water, and then when the lead cooled, the shapes of the lead would tell you your fortune for the coming year. Everyone tried it, but I don't know if any of the predictions ever came true.

When Christmas got close, my father cut a Christmas tree from the woods and brought it into the house for decorating. And we always had Finnish foods, especially for holidays. We had rice pudding with fruit sauce, *nisua*, and *lipeäkala* [dried cod]. In the old days we'd take a large, dried codfish and soak it in water for one week. We'd have to change the water every day. Then the fish was soaked in a solution of raw soda ashes and water until the meat looked shiny. Then we had to soak it in fresh water for seven more days, changing the water each day. Finally, on Christmas Eve we'd cook the fish and serve it with a rich sauce. It was a very important part of our Christmas meal.

We went to church always on Christmas, and every Sunday, too. We went to the original Conneaut Evangelical Lutheran Church on Broad Street until the new Good Shepherd Lutheran was built on Lake Road. In the old days, there were two separate services: the Finnish service at 9:30 and the English service an hour later. I was confirmed when I was fifteen. I studied the Bible for a year before that, and I wore a white communion dress on the Sunday I was confirmed.

When I was a teenager, I wore black stockings and boots and cotton dresses. I had long straight hair that I called "Finn hair." Sometimes I braided it on the sides and tied it back, and sometimes I curled it by rolling it up with strips of rags. Then, in the 1920s, when the other girls were bobbing their hair, I did too, and I wore those flapper dresses.

Silent movies were popular then, and I went to a lot of them. In those days they had a person in the movie theater who played a piano right along with the movie.

We had the only sauna in the neighborhood, so we had a lot of company on Saturday evenings. I prepared coffee bread and cakes for all of our visitors. I was always up late on Saturday nights to help entertain guests, but I'd get up early Sunday morning for church.

My mother died in 1932 so I had to take over all the housekeeping and cooking and help run the farm. I got up early to help milk more than fifty cows. That took an hour, even with a milking machine, then the milk was piped into a cooling tank. I was so busy there wasn't time to think about marriage.

I remember my father telling me how he read letters in Italian for an Italian man he worked with. My father didn't speak Italian, and he didn't understand what he was reading, but the Italian could understand. People of all nationalities worked together, but Finnish parents wanted their children to marry within their same nationality. They didn't approve if a son or daughter wanted to marry an Italian or a Hungarian.

I think there are many things for the Finns to be proud of. They have always been a hard-working people, and even when times were hard they would rather work than take a handout. And the Finns have always been a very literate people. In the old days in Finland, you had to be able to read the Bible and answer questions about it even before you could get married.

I traveled to Finland in 1980, and I was surprised when I saw all the changes. It's become such a modern country. Everything is electronic, and women dress in the latest fashions. It's very different from when I was a little girl. Then there were very distinct class differences, and so many people were poor.

After my dad and brother died, I still have some things that came from Finland: this old violin . . . and this wall clock was a wedding gift to my parents from my dad's father.

Verna's later years were spent in the assisted-living portion of Villa at the Lake, in Conneaut. When Verna was interviewed and asked the secret of her longevity, she replied, "I never smoked, never drank, and never got married!" Verna Warpula died at the age of ninety-four on December 31, 2005.

Lempi Kajander Kaihlanen

My oldest brother was first to come here in 1901. I was born 1900, February 19, and was one year old when he left. My brother live on farm in Dorset [Ashtabula County], and he was divorced with two little boys at home. He want Grandma to come take care of his boys, so I came with Mother and Father in 1920 when I was twenty. I didn't care to come—no American fever—but my mother was crying, so I made up my mind and came and had to leave all my friends there. We came on new and beautiful ship and took two weeks, but I was sick. I had to throw up when I heard the dinner bell. I didn't eat much.

I was glad when we seen New York and Statue of Liberty. Ellis Island was terrible place. We came on Labor Day, and they weren't working. So we had to stay there all night and sleep on a spring and nothing on it. "Oh," I thought, "that's America?" I couldn't sleep, and we had to wait for my brother to get us out of there. I was glad to get out.

My father, Otto Kajander, was fish dealer in Voikka, Finland, and had never lived on farm before. He had his own business and didn't know how to farm and take care of horse and cow. So my father and mother [Marja Sutela] became homesick, and they went back to Finland after staying here for ten or eleven months, but I stayed.

My first job was maid at National Hotel—across from depot. I was dishwasher. I teach myself English from newspapers, and my brother explain for me. I went grade school [in Finland]; that's all they had then. So I try to learn to talk [English], but never learn good, anyways.

I remember Yellow Hall on Lake Avenue. I didn't go to Socialist meetings there—just dancing. Sovinto was really beautiful hall; they had dancing and plays. I met my husband [John Oscar Kaihlanen] at Sovinto, where he belonged [a member]. Oscar was born in Mikkili, Finland, March 17, 1901. He came to America when he was six months old. We got married on September 6, 1923, and we move to Detroit. Oscar work at White Motor Company. Our daughter [Eleanor Ann] was born there in 1926.

When Depression came, Oscar lost his job and we move back to Ashtabula. We live with Oscar's parents on Morton Drive. He work part time on the Lakes—sailing in summer. I sewed for two tailors: Kosonen, on Bridge Street, and Saarinen was on Morton Drive, and I get five dollars a week. Then my husband dug ditches when WPA [Works Progress Administration] started. We had to get transfers from bank to pay for milk and food. The amount was on paper script, and it would pay the landlord, then the script would go back to bank.

Now we have paved roads and no trains anymore. Lots of things change little by little every year, and you change with it.

Oscar was caretaker for few years at Sovinto. We live upstairs on third floor—up to heaven. I remember Hukkari's and Brant's [grocers], but I didn't have to go grocery store. The grocer came to house in morning and brought groceries in afternoon. To order was easier. The Humina Band had lots of young men. I remember Wahlstrom, but I never met him. They practice behind hall. In 1934–36, they still practice and we could hear. Eleanor was four years old when she recite Finnish poem for children's program at Sovinto.

Oscar then worked for dock company—Ashtabula and Buffalo Docks—for almost thirty years. We bought farm in 1948 on Merchants Avenue [Gerald Road] in Saybrook. We sold eggs and chickens.

We went to Finland two times. First time in 1925, and last time I see my parents alive. My mother died when she was eighty-five. She fell on ice and broke hip. That time you couldn't fix them. I have lace tablecloth my mother made, and I bring back two copper teakettles. We flew over again in 1959. It had changed over there; lots of it for better. More schools and lots of more-educated people, just like here. Helsinki was cleaner there than here. Years go by and I want to go back, but you couldn't. So life has changed, and I still am homesick, but I don't really have anybody [in Finland].

When Mr. Kaihlanen retire, we sold farm and build new house next to my daughter and son-in-law. My husband died in 1980.

Lempi lived alone until shortly before her hundredth birthday, when she became unsteady on her feet. She then moved in with her daughter and son-in-law, Eleanor and Lawson Stevenson, where she maintained her good health and outlived her sister and three brothers, who had also immigrated here. One brother remained in Finland. Lempi died on June 27, 2003, at the age of 103. She left her daughter, four grandchildren, and four great-grandchildren. Eleanor contributed her mother's longevity to her sisu. Eleanor also said when she used to fuss over her mother, she would say, "I use to be the mother."

Eleanor Talja Andrews

My father, Kalle Talja, lived in Suoniemi, and my mother, Fannie Aalto, was from Tampere. They left Finland in 1924, and I'm not sure why, except that my grandfather expected my dad to take over the family farm while his older brother went to a university and became a teacher. Anyway, they went first to Canada and were married there. Then they crossed over from Ontario to Detroit, Michigan. At the railroad station they were asked where they wanted to go. Because they didn't know anyone in the United States, they put some money on the counter and asked, "Where will this take us?" They were told that amount would take them to Ashtabula, Ohio, and they bought the tickets. Luckily, when they got off the train and walked to Lake Avenue, they turned left and went into the area known then as Forty Acres, where many Finns and Italians lived. There they met a Finnish man, and it was he who helped them find an apartment on West Twenty-eighth Street.

A few days later my father was hired by the New York Central Railroad, where he stayed for thirty-one years. He was a track laborer and, during winters, often had to work through the night to clear snow and ice from the switches. I remember Dad coming home with his clothes and eyebrows covered with ice. The other workers were Italian and had never heard the name, Kalle, so they called him Karlo instead, which was easier for them to pronounce. Karlo was the name used on all his checks and documents, but he was still Kalle to everyone else.

But the Talja name was never changed or altered. In fact, the name can be traced back to 1737, when the Talja homestead was built. This home was declared a national landmark on August 8, 1971, by President Kekkonen. One half of it became a museum while the other half still remains occupied by a Talja descendant.

I was born on July 12, 1927, when my parents were still living on West Twenty-eighth. My mother went to a maternity hospital on West Eighth

Street, where Dr. Collander, who delivered me, had his office. I was to be their only child and grew up in the Forty Acres region. I attended Station Avenue School and couldn't speak English at first, but I had a wonderful teacher who helped me. Yet I remember another teacher who asked, "How do you pronounce your last name, dear? It's such a strange name." And I was to bring home As—no question about it.

Dad didn't lose his job during the Depression, but his hours were cut, and some weeks he worked only two days. My mother always supplemented his income by cleaning offices and houses. When I got a little older, I sometimes got up at five o'clock and went with her to help. Believe me, cleaning spittoons wasn't my favorite job! And I remember once during those years, when I was in the bathroom, I called out to my mother, "Do you think next payday we could buy toilet paper?"

When I was about eight years old, the circus came to town, so my father and I walked about a quarter of a mile to join the crowd. During the performance a tiger somehow got loose, and that created quite a ruckus when people scrambled to get away from that area. My father suddenly realized I wasn't there, and he began searching and searching. Finally, he gave up and walked home, and there I was. Well, he really gave me a bawling out, but when he finished his scolding, I said, defensively, "In a time like that, it's eveyone for himself!"

My mother raised a garden and cooked traditional Finnish dishes such as *nisua, kropsua,* and *vispii puuro* [a whipped pudding, usually made with grape juice]. She also made the best-ever swiss steak, which, of course, wasn't Finnish. And she sold advertising space for a Finnish-language newspaper, the *Raivaaja,* and submitted articles of local interest that they published.

I always helped with household chores, gardening, and canning, but I wore hand-me-down clothes. They were lovely clothes, though, from Lillian Wuorimaki. Her father owned a prosperous plumbing business, and they had a beautiful brick home on Walnut Boulevard.

Even though my parents both worked hard, we had some fun times, too. We belonged to a Finnish hall on the corner of West Twenty-sixth Street and Lake Avenue where they had a library, a theater, and where dances were held and plays performed. My mother enjoyed acting and went along with others to perform plays for other Finnish organizations in Fairport Harbor and Cleveland. Of course, we went to the public sauna on West Thirtieth Street, and we celebrated *Juhannus* along with other Finnish friends. We hand made ornaments for our Christmas tree and exchanged small gifts. We occasionally attended services at Bethany Lutheran Church, but we weren't members. My father decided he'd had enough of church in Finland because his father was so strict about churchgoing.

We never owned a car. We walked to the grocery store in our neighborhood, which was Italian owned, even though our languages were very different. The Italians and Finns got along real well, though. In fact, whenever there was a death or illness in someone's family, the Italian neighbor would bring over some spaghetti, or a Finnish neighbor would give the Italian a coffee bread. We couldn't carry on a conversation, so we just smiled a lot. And we walked to the movie theaters uptown or at the harbor, which were quite a hike from West Twenty-sixth Street and from Station Avenue where we lived later. Dad had a railroad employee's pass, and we took occasional rides to Cleveland or Erie where we would shop and sightsee.

I remember coming home from the movies on Sunday, December 7, 1941, and my mother told me Pearl Harbor had been bombed by the Japanese. All during World War II, students bought and sold stamps, and when a stamp book was filled it would buy a savings bond with the money going toward the war effort. Then rationing was begun. Ration stamps were issued to everyone to limit the buying of goods like meat, sugar, and shoes, with the price of each item not to exceed the stamp's value.

After my 1945 graduation from Ashtabula High School, I couldn't afford to go to college, so three days later I had my first job in the office of the Illuminating Company. My salary was seventeen dollars a week, and I was happy to get it.

I wore a lovely gray suit instead of a wedding gown when I married Warren Andrews in 1947. Our first apartment was on Park Avenue, which was ironic because that house was on the future site where the Ashtabula County Savings & Loan would be built and where Warren would work for thirty-three years. The first house we bought was on West Fifty-eighth Street, and from there we moved to Elk Drive, then to Locust Drive, on the lakefront. Our first son, Mark, was born in 1950; then Charles (Chuck) in 1952; and Susan in 1956. Susan is the only member of our family who has traveled to Finland. Her 1974 trip included a visit to the old Talja homestead in Suoniemi.

My mother always wanted to buy their own home, but Dad just refused to go into debt for one. Then, when Mother died, Dad came to live with us until he died, twenty-seven years later, at the age of eighty-nine. I do believe he was a positive influence on our children, though. He was a model of integrity and upheld good work ethics. He was an avid reader, as well, and kept informed with current events. I wish the younger generations would respect their elders more and learn from them; they have so much to offer by way of experience and example.

I continued to work while my children were growing up. I was secretary at Windermere Elementary School for six years and a secretary at Harbor High School for twenty-six years. It was disturbing for me to witness changes in the family structure throughout the years; for instance, one out of three Ashtabula households had a single parent, whereas the national average was one out of four. More often, guidance was left to the schools.

I served twelve years as a "Model United Nations" advisor. Then, in 1993—my last year as advisor—I accompanied members of this student organization to New York City. We visited the World Trade Center, and the following day we were in the United Nations building when we heard the chilling news that a bomb had gone off in the basement of the Trade Center, where we had been just the day before. The next day we had to wait on a bus while the tunnels were being inspected and weren't allowed to travel until the tunnels were announced "all clear." Even so, the tunnels appeared ominous.

No, I never visited Finland, but we had relatives visit here. My cousin, Ritva Salonen, was a member of the Finnish rhythmic gymnastic team that competed in the summer Olympics held in Italy in 1960. The teams, men's and women's, toured the United States and performed in the Harbor High School gymnasium to a standing-room-only crowd. Then another cousin, Marja Leena Talvitie, visited us for one summer. She came to improve her conversational English after eight years of classroom study. She sat in on classes at Kent-Ashtabula and worked in a local restaurant. She has since worked for the Finnish State Department at various posts: Dublin, the United Nations, and currently in Paris. Her daughter, Elina, was graduated from high school in Dublin at St. Andrews while her mother was stationed there. Elina wrote her international baccalaureate extended essay in her senior year (1991/1992), describing the Russian February Manifesto of 1899, which created increased efforts by Russia to undermine Finnish autonomy. This prompted the Finns to write the Great Address, signed by a half-million Finns, protesting this oppression. A group of representative Finns was chosen to deliver the Great Address to Czar Nicholas II. My grandfather Talja was one of these men, but the czar refused to accept the Great Address from the delegation. Elina's essay gives a detailed account of the Manifesto and the Great Address, and her essay was subsequently accepted for publication in the *Concord Review* [summer 1993: 99–124].

Eleanor was named "Citizen of the Year" in 1989, and was further honored when she was inducted into Ashtabula High School's Hall of Fame in 2001. After Warren's death in 1999, and the sale of their family home, Eleanor moved in 2001 to smaller quarters in Willowbrook where she stays involved with family and friends and, like her father, is an avid reader who keeps up with current affairs in the community as well as in the world. Eleanor has seven grandchildren and one great-granddaughter.

Eino Sinkkonen

I was born in Jakkima on the Karelian side, now Russia, on April 17, 1918. After the war, I lived in several places, and last place was Varkaus. My father had died, so I had three half brothers when my mother got married again. Our family was poor and didn't have anything special, but we got along somehow. My stepfather was a shoemaker and a chimney sweeper.

In 1932 and 1933, I had a job working at a private home. It was like a drugstore, and I helped out with the drugs. Most of the drugs were liquid, so there was a lot of work to do. I made distilled water and then mixed it with alcohol. I took care of the basement and all janitorial work. It was a big place and seventeen people lived there.

I went into the Finnish army on November 17, 1939, which was my name day. [Finns celebrate name days instead of their actual birthday.] The war started [with Russia] on November 30, so I was in the army less than two weeks when the Winter War started. I had training all the way to January 15, and then I was taken to the front lines. The war lasted three months, but I was actually at the front for two months. I was an artillery man. I still have some ribbons with medals. Then the Continuation War started in 1941, and that's when I went to medic school for six months—between time. So I changed jobs. I wasn't an artillery man in a combat group, but a medic isn't the best job in the world. You might get ten or fifteen patients in a few seconds and then you have to know what to do.

I had some gardener training before the war, but I couldn't go to this school because of the war, but after the war I took several short courses, whatever was available. So I had three years of training and worked in different places as a gardener.

I married Sylvia Hukala in February 1944. We had one daughter, Leena, born 1945. I rented a greenhouse business in Varkaus, but first I built the house, close to the Russian border. I was working for a Sami [Lapp] congregation. I was paid by them and—how to say—like a grave digger and gardener. I was two and a half to three years on that job, but then it was too close to the Russian border, and I had been working twenty-four hours a day. There wasn't any possibility to get a better job, so I sold my house in 1949 and left the area.

After the war I took drama classes in Kangasala and worked there at the young people's place, and I took the drama course for the Tampere Theatre group. I even started a little community theater where I had built my house. Then when I came to Varkaus they had a theater, and I was over three years there in many plays. I didn't have trouble memorizing the lines. The trouble was the other people couldn't remember their lines and you just had to get used to it.

I left Finland in April 1955. The boat was a Swedish line, and we left from Stockholm. We stopped at West Germany, Bremerhaven, and getting more passengers again from there, then to Halifax and New York. We had a nice time on that boat. My [sailing] companion was from Canada, and he was a pretty good guy, but he wore a union suit on and it was no color—just gray. I think it was so dirty that it didn't have any white left. I told him one morning, "Why don't you take that union suit and put it to the end of the rope and throw it to the sea after the boat? Then it would be clean when we get to New York." He took his union suit off and we went up to the deck and it was little bit cold wind blowing on. After a while he said, "I have to go and put that suit back on again." He was a funny guy!

I thought I'd change my name to Sinko when I got my citizenship, but it had been Sinkkonen since 1630 in the church records, so I thought I'm going to keep my Finnish name.

I went first to Erie because my sponsors, Arvo and Hilma Viitala, lived there. I stayed with them but I couldn't get a job in Erie. Then I saw a job advertised in the *Star Beacon*. The Yoder Brothers in Ashtabula needed a man. They were the chrysanthemum growers, and they leased all their greenhouses. I was working four and a half years, and then I got a promotion and was a foreman after that.

My wife and daughter came here thirteen months later. The first home I bought here was in 1957 on Summer Avenue. There was still both halls here, and there was a little going on, like dances, but I was more into the Kaleva Lodge and I joined it. I joined the first year at Bethany Lutheran Church, and I sang with the Ashtabula Town Choir the first year in 1955. I sang the first time in English at the dedication of the church organ with the Town Choir. I have a picture of it. I sang only one year in the Town Choir, because Kaarlo Mackey [the director] got killed in a car accident. I liked him. He was a perfectionist; he knew his stuff. But I sang in the Bethany church choir several times and on different occasions. I sang solos for the Finnish church services, and for many church funerals.

In 1961 I started working at Rockwell Standard, and then it was changed to Rockwell International. I worked fifteen years in the brake-division factory. After I retired from there, I worked one and a half years in a drugstore.

After my first wife died, I married Martha Juhola, and we lived on Lyndon Avenue. Martha was a registered nurse at Ashtabula General Hospital, and she was a Finn, but born in this country. After Martha died, April 13, 1998, when she was eighty-four, I moved to Haywood Beach in Saybrook Township.

Eino sold his Haywood Beach home, along with its beautifully landscaped lot, and moved to Lake Worth, Florida, in 2001, where he resides in the Finnish Rest Home. His daughter Leena Skiba lives in North Carolina and has two daughters, Maija and Amy.

Kalle and Fannie (Aalto) Talja emigrated from Finland in 1924 and knew no one in Ashtabula when they first arrived. This photo was taken in 1925 to send to family left behind. (Photo courtesy of Eleanor Talja Andrews)

City Savings and Loan board of directors in 1927 on Bridge Street, Ashtabula Harbor. Left to right: Lars Husgard, Henry Waivala, Walter Lakari, Charles Hukari, Simon Huhta, Charles Potti, John Glantz, John Lundi, and John Purtilo. The sign on the right reads: "Finnish Savings and Loan" to accommodate bank customers who spoke only Finnish. (Photo donated to FACC by Elaine Richardson)

Thirteen Sippola siblings gathered at their mother's home, ca. 1929. Left to right: Emmi, Anna, Sylvia, Martha, Leona, Ida, Virginia, Isaac, Hilda, Jennie, Mary, Elizabeth, John, and mother, Kaisa (Katherine). (Family photo)

Jerry Peterson and mother, Martha. Jerry was home on leave from the navy on this 1944 Easter Sunday in Fairport Harbor. (Photo courtesy of Jerry Peterson)

Facing page: John Karbacka, lieutenant in the U.S. Coast Guard. This 1943 photo was taken near Sault Sainte Marie, Michigan. (Photo courtesy of Elizabeth Karbacka)

In 1951 the Laituri siblings traveled from California, Massachusetts, Michigan, and Ohio to celebrate their parents' fiftieth wedding anniversary. Top row: Matthew, Mauno John, Melvin, and Mickey; center: Milma, Mauri, Martha, Martin, and Marie; seated: Antti and Maria (ages 72 and 70, respectively). (Photo courtesy of M. John Laituri)

Jim and Marilyn Salo at their wedding reception in the fellowship hall of the first Bethany Lutheran Church in Ashtabula Harbor, May 8, 1954. (Photo courtesy of Marilyn Salo)

Representatives of the Associated Country Women of the World, on tour of the United States, visited a northern Ashtabula County farm in the mid 1950s. Verna Warpula, far right; Anne Laakson, center, was from Finland. The other three women are unidentified. (Photo courtesy of FACC)